EXPLORING

VANCOUVER

EXPLORING

VANCOUVER

THE

Text by Harold Kalman, Ron Phillips, and Robin Ward

ESSENTIAL

Photographs and book design by Robin Ward

ARCHITECTURAL

Additional photography by Ron Phillips

GUIDE

UBC Press / Vancouver

ISBN 0-7748-0410-6

Canadian Cataloguing in Publication Data

Kalman, Harold, 1943-
  Exploring Vancouver

Includes bibliographical references and index.
ISBN 0-7748-0410-6

1. Architecture – British Columbia – Vancouver –
Guidebooks. 2. Historic buildings – British
Columbia – Vancouver – Guidebooks. 3. Buildings –
British Columbia – Vancouver – Guidebooks. I.
Phillips, Ronald A., 1944- II. Ward, Robin, 1950-
III. Title.

NA747.V3K34 1993   720'.9711'33   C92-091846-8

Publication of this book was made possible by ongoing support from
the Canada Council, the Province of British Columbia Cultural Services Branch,
and the Department of Communications of Canada.

UBC Press
University of British Columbia
6344 Memorial Rd
Vancouver, BC V6T 1Z2
(604) 822-3259
Fax: (604) 822-6083

Illustrations:
Page 1: Marine Building (detail)
Page 2: Seymour Building

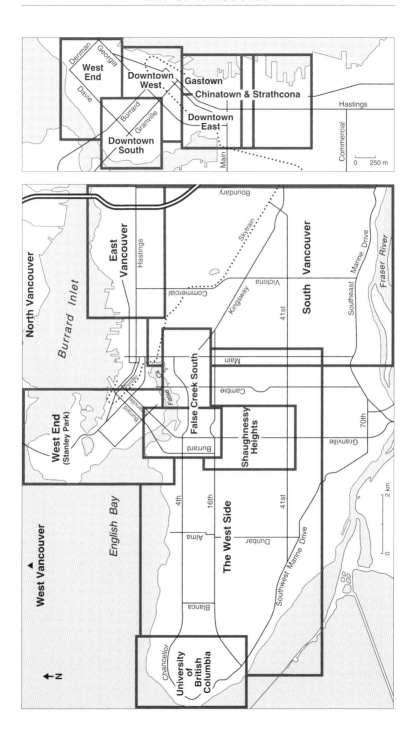

CONTENTS

An art deco tour de force

Marine Building

INTRODUCTION

I F, on a clear day, you approach Vancouver along Granville Street, you will be struck not so much by the city as by its setting. The sudden view north as Granville Street crests Shaughnessy Heights presents a stunning juxtaposition of the city centre clustered with towers and the North Shore mountains beyond. Even in the canyons of downtown you cannot entirely escape the exhilarating presence of the wild periphery with which the city collides.

The natural setting can be something of a distraction when looking at the city's architecture. Vancouver looks so good that it is easy to overlook its buildings. But there is much in Vancouver to admire. Rows of colourful frame houses and Italianate commercial façades reflect pioneering optimism. Stout Edwardian banks, defiantly and incongruously neoclassical, and gracious revivalist houses reveal the accumulation of capital and the growing sophistication of the city's architects. More recently, the flowering West Coast style has produced buildings which are exceptionally sympathetic to the scenery in which they are set. One of the best, the UBC Museum of Anthropology, is a work of inter-

national repute. In a different manner, but with equal conviction, the art deco Marine Building, among others, achieves a similar status.

In the last two decades, the flight from the city which character-ized the fifties and sixties has largely been reversed. The densely packed streets of Gastown, Downtown, and the West End are now alive with traditional city life and character. The redevelopment of False Creek South has been a trend-setting exercise in inner-city revitaliza-tion. High density is increasingly seen as more efficient in terms of land use and public transportation than sprawling suburbs and, architec-turally, the traditional city offers more creative potential. But Vancou-verites are used to seascapes, mountain views, and open space – some critics have called Vancouver a setting in search of a city. The challenge for developers, architects, and planners is to avoid despoiling the for-mer while enriching the latter.

As the city has matured, it has acquired an appreciation of its ar-chitectural heritage. Youthful vigour and laissez-faire development pre-viously ignored this enriching and stabilizing factor in city life. Growing,

left: *Ebullient beaux-arts stonework decorates the former General Post Office at the Sinclair Centre.*

right: *Granville Island's industrial heritage is sympathetically reflected in new construction.*

if belated, concern for the city's past is now being shown, and the re-use of old buildings is encouraged (Granville Island and the Sinclair Centre are exemplary in this respect). But 'heritage' can have its drawbacks. There is the possibility of a 'heritage chill' developing. Exciting modern work fails to emerge in a climate where developers and architects feel that planning permission will be more easily gained by playing safe with heritage pastiche rather than with a contemporary alternative. But the desire to conserve the past and also achieve an innovative contemporary architecture has produced intriguing solutions, and some, like the Four Sisters Housing Co-operative, are particularly successful. In Vancouver, the dialectics of urbanism and the natural setting, and preservation and innovation, are forces that continue to shape the city's development and its architecture.

In *Exploring Vancouver*, architecture is taken in its broadest sense to include the whole of the man-made environment – the buildings, gardens, monuments, parks, and streets that make up the physical structure of the city. This book is also a history of Vancouver through its

left: *The muscular industrial classicism of Ballantyne Pier on the waterfront*

right: *The award-winning Four Sisters Housing Co-operative, an exemplary inner city project developed by the Downtown Eastside Residents Association*

architecture. This history is presented geographically, and, to an extent, chronologically, with the development of the city from its historical centre in Gastown mirrored in the arrangement of this guide.

Entries were selected with several criteria in mind. Many were chosen for architectural reasons – for excellence of design, as representing a particular style or method of construction, or for visual interest, curiosity, or even ugliness. Others were chosen because of their cultural, historical, or social significance. There were often differing opinions on the merits of particular buildings, which is to be expected given the authors' different backgrounds in fine arts, architectural history, and urban geography; but, since this is a group project, a consensus was reached on a selection that represents the strengths of each of these points of view. This does not mean that personal favourites were omitted, and strong enthusiasm from any one of the authors was considered a decisive factor.

In preparing the book the city was divided into its component areas and each author assumed responsibility for the selection of build-

ings and the writing of the text for the entries within assigned areas. Gastown, Shaughnessy, False Creek South, and East Vancouver were prepared by Ron Phillips. Harold Kalman was responsible for South Vancouver, the West Side, and the University of British Columbia. Robin Ward covered the West End, Chinatown and Strathcona, Downtown East, Downtown West, and Downtown South. Robin Ward and Ron Phillips jointly prepared the North Vancouver and West Vancouver sections. Simon Fraser University, although it falls outside the overall area covered by this book, is included in the East Vancouver section. The authors are aware that, in order to keep the book to a manageable size, many buildings which might have been included have been omitted or may have been overlooked. Work in progress, especially the Pacific Place and Coal Harbour megaprojects, has only been considered in passing.

Dates given for construction are considered accurate to within one year unless prefaced by circa (abbreviated c.). When a building has been known by more than one name through the years, the least am-

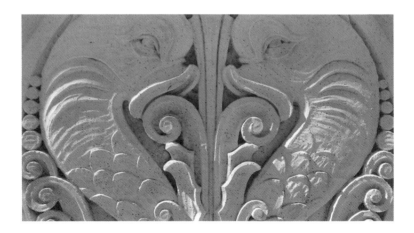

biguous one is given in the heading and others are listed in the text. Private houses are identified with their original occupant, who may or may not be the present one. Where the information was available, the name of the architect has been included for each building.

A map of the city showing the fourteen areas covered in the book appears on page 5. More detailed area maps are at the back of the book (pages 265-80). These maps show the location of featured buildings covered in the text, with map numbers corresponding to text entry numbers. Arrows with numbers indicate buildings which lie beyond the margins of the map. For those less familiar with architectural terms there is a glossary at the back of the book. There is also an illustrated guide to the architectural styles most commonly found in Vancouver. This is included to help the reader identify and loosely date other buildings of interest.

The reader should note that unless the public nature of a building is obvious or specifically mentioned in the text, none of the buildings shown in this book are open to the public. In a few instances, buildings

left: *Art deco panels decorate the Federal Building at the Sinclair Centre.*

right: *Edwardian craftsman style homes enrich West Side streetscapes (1700-block Dunbar Street).*

which are not readily visible from the public roadway are listed. This has been done only with the permission of owners and where significance demands inclusion. The reader should not trespass to gain a better view.

Special thanks are due to Holly Keller-Brohman at UBC Press for her editorial input, Meg Stanley of Commonwealth Historic Resource Management for her research, and to Mary Shaughnessy for preliminary assistance. Our warmest thanks also go to Marco D'Agostino, Barry Downs, Robert Lemon, and Gary Penway for their specialized knowledge and advice. We are also indebted to the many architects, builders, and developers who took the time to describe their work and to the many individuals who shared their knowledge of their homes and places of work.

Research for this book was assisted by a grant from the Architectural Institute of British Columbia, while Novam Development and Concord Pacific Developments provided financial assistance towards photography costs.

Fanciful carved capitals

enliven warehouse façades.

Greenshields Building

Area One **GASTOWN**

O N a drizzly September day in 1867, a former river pilot named John Deighton landed on the south shore of Burrard Inlet to open a saloon for the employees of the Hastings Mill. Situated among a grove of maple trees at today's Water and Carrall streets, 'Gassy Jack' Deighton's saloon (his name derived from his reputation as a windbag) formed the nucleus of a rowdy settlement that came to be known as Gassy's Town or Gastown. The new townsite was surveyed in 1870 and officially named Granville.

The future of the town was assured a decade later when the Canadian Pacific Railway decided to extend its transcontinental line to the south shore of Burrard Inlet, and in 1886 the town of Granville was incorporated as the City of Vancouver. The name, said to have been chosen by the CPR's William Van Horne, honours Captain George Vancouver, who had charted Burrard Inlet in 1792 for the Royal Navy.

Vancouver's role as a shipping and distribution centre was reflected in the warehouses and wholesale stores that lined Water Street; Cordova Street became the principal commercial thoroughfare, with an

electric streetcar line as early as 1890. Residential areas began to de-velop outside Gastown to the east and west of the city as the forest was cleared.

A severe depression struck in 1892 but ended six years later with the rush for gold in the Klondike. Many of Gastown's large commercial blocks and hotels were built with gold rush money. The boom contin-ued almost uninterrupted until the First World War. But between 1908 and 1913, when Vancouver underwent its period of greatest early growth, the centre of commercial activity had shifted west to the Eastern Business District. The north side of Water Street continued as the city's wholesale grocery district well into the 1940s when the shift from railways to trucking made distribution from suburban warehouses more economical. For nearly half a century Gastown steadily declined. Ironically, the lack of economic activity served a useful end; little new construction took place, but at the same time few old buildings were demolished or modernized.

The revitalization of Gastown began in the late 1960s. Old build-

left: *Rusticated stonework adds texture to the façade of this former Hudson's Bay Company warehouse.*

right: *Telegraph poles, overhead wires (long removed from Water Street), and a motley collection of façades lend Alexander Street a residual workaday character.*

ings found new owners and were rehabilitated as shops and restaurants. In February 1971 the government of British Columbia designated most of Gastown and adjacent Chinatown as historic areas, thereby preventing demolition and controlling restoration and development. City planners developed a 'beautification' program in which streets and alleys were improved and landscaped, and electrical wires were buried.

Gastown today is a lively mixture of shops, restaurants, studios, privately developed condominiums, and social housing. Like any district that has undergone rapid and drastic change, Gastown has been the subject of praise and the object of criticism. 'Gentrification' has meant the influx of new people, rising rents, and major dislocation for the area's existing residents. Many moved eastward to Strathcona and many have been housed in new rent-controlled housing. The Downtown Eastside Residents Association (DERA) has championed the original Gastown residents through the development of such social housing projects as the award-winning Four Sisters Housing Co-operative on Powell Street.

1
HOTEL EUROPE
43 Powell Street
Parr & Fee 1908-9

Angelo Colari, an Italian-Canadian hotelier, erected this flatiron building, the best commercial hotel in town. It was the earliest reinforced concrete structure in Vancouver and the first fireproof hotel in western Canada. With its flat brick walls and sparse decoration, it contrasts with the more ornate hotels on Water Street. The lobby retains its original tile, marble, and brass fittings.

2
1 Alexander Street
N.S. Hoffar 1898

This warehouse originally served the ship chandlery and hardware business of Thomas Dunn, a member of Vancouver's first city council. Dunn retained the prominent architect N.S. Hoffar who, a decade earlier, had designed the Lonsdale Block on Cordova for Dunn and his partner Jonathan Miller. Fine brickwork and decorated cast-iron pillars complement this handsome Romanesque revival façade.

3
BYRNES BLOCK
2 Water Street
Elmer H. Fisher 1886-7

A statue of Gassy Jack Deighton gazes across Maple Tree Square in front of this fine Italianate commercial block – originally the Alhambra Hotel – which stands on the site of his second saloon. Its ornate window pediments, top-floor pilasters, and decorated cornice all boast of the relative opulence of the former hotel, one of the few then charging more than a dollar a night.

4

SECOND FERGUSON BLOCK
200 Carrall Street
begun 1886

As part of the agreement that brought the terminus of the transcontinental railway to Vancouver, the CPR acquired large tracts of land on Burrard Inlet and around False Creek. This building contained the CPR land offices. Stilted arched windows with incised flourishes and keystones are imaginatively grouped in pairs on the Powell Street façade, which is capped with a bracketed cornice.

5

OPPENHEIMER BROTHERS STORE
102 Powell Street
N.S. Hoffar 1891

The Oppenheimer brothers arrived in BC from Bavaria in 1856 and soon became the leading businessmen of Yale, BC, during the Cariboo gold rush. Two of the five brothers, David and Isaac, settled in Vancouver. Among their many enterprises was a wholesale grocery in this brick warehouse (rehabilitated as a recording studio in 1991 by Bryan Adams). David Oppenheimer was Vancouver's second mayor, from 1888 to 1891.

6

FLECK BROTHERS BUILDING
103 Powell Street
1908

The odd shape of this building, now a rent-controlled housing project, and several other buildings on the eastern edge of Gastown, including the Merchants' Bank (95), derives from a CPR spur line that ran from Burrard Inlet to the roundhouse (188) and marshalling yards at False Creek. A small courtyard has been added in the triangular space left when the tracks were removed in 1931.

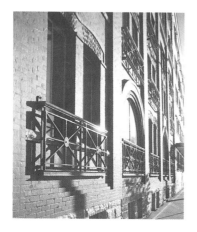

7
FOUR SISTERS HOUSING CO-OPERATIVE
133 Powell Street
Davidson & Yuen 1987

Developed by the Downtown Eastside Residents Association, the award-winning Four Sisters is social housing at its best. An imaginative combination of new wood-frame and masonry construction and a rehabilitated existing warehouse (on Alexander Street), the resident-run co-operative has an urbane, European feel that fits seamlessly into the Gastown environment.

8
SALVATION ARMY HARBOUR LIGHT CENTRE
119-29 East Cordova Street
Davidson & Yuen 1987

The architectural world has long debated issues of originality versus imitation. Where buildings like Gaslight Square (13) introduce modernist features, this building, like the Four Sisters Housing Co-op (7), explores postmodern possibilites of reinvented period details and styles: its rhythm, scale, and vocabulary are taken from the urban landscape around it.

9
GRAND HOTEL
26 Water Street
c. 1890

The south side of Water Street was Vancouver's first hotel district; the north side of the street was often under water at high tide until it was filled in by the CPR around 1890. The Grand Hotel is a good example of the popular Italianate style. Arches of contrasting colours and shapes cap the upper floor windows.

10
TERMINUS HOTEL
30 Water Street
Bunning & Kelso 1886
A curved pediment crowns the façade of this attractive small hotel, named for Vancouver's selection as terminus of the CPR. The upper storeys feature projecting bay windows, a common local architectural feature that came to Vancouver from San Francisco. Despite the individuality of its detail, the Terminus harmonizes well in scale and texture with its neighbours to the east.

11
THIRD MALKIN WAREHOUSE
57 Water Street
Parr & Fee 1907-12
William Harold Malkin, a successful wholesale grocer who began as a tea importer and later became mayor of Vancouver, built three warehouses on Water Street within eight years. The simple façade and heavy cornice are typical of Parr & Fee's commercial buildings – note the same architects' Hotel Europe (1), for example.

12
DOMINION HOTEL
92 Water Street
E.G. Guenther 1900-1
The Dominion Hotel, originally the Sherdahl Block, shared this building with a ground-floor department store. A fine example of the Italianate style, its colourful arches and pilasters make its neighbours seem dull by comparison. Awkward brick arches, which were inserted at street level in a 1969 alteration, have been replaced with a much more attractive and appropriate wood-panelled fascia.

13
GASLIGHT SQUARE
131 Water Street
Henriquez & Todd 1974-5
After the demise of Project 200 (see 27) and the bulldoze-and-rebuild philosophy it represented, Marathon Realty made a philosophical about-face and built Gaslight Square, the first new structure to recognize Gastown's distinctive character. With its bay windows, brick walls, and layered courtyard, Gaslight Square consciously mirrors the vocabulary and scale of the other buildings along Water Street but in a modern manner.

14
LECKIE BUILDING
170 Water Street
1908
The steel rods which run diagonally across the ground-floor windows to the top storey are part of an innovative system of steel cross-bracing, posts, and beams which upgrade this former bootery and garment factory to current seismic standards. Novam Development won a 1992 City of Vancouver Heritage Award for the structural upgrading of the building (Vladimir Vit, architect, and Gower Yeung & Associates, engineers, 1991).

15
EDWARD HOTEL
300 Water Street
1906
On this site stood the Regina Hotel, the only building in Gastown to survive the fire of 1886. A small group of men trapped in the building fought to save their lives and managed to save the building as well. In 1906 the Regina was demolished – by the wrecker's hammer – and replaced by the Edward Hotel. The upper floors feature rusticated stone piers and horizontal floral bands.

16
GASTOWN STEAM CLOCK
Water and Cambie streets
Raymond L. Saunders 1977

The world's first steam clock, by horologist and sculptor Raymond Saunders, sounds the notes of London's Big Ben on its five steam whistles. Powered by a single-cylinder engine and driven by a fascinating chain and ball-weight drive that is visible through the clock's glass sides, it draws crowds of fascinated tourists for its quarter-hourly performance.

17
McCLARY MANUFACTURING COMPANY WAREHOUSE
305 Water Street
Hooper & Watkins 1899

The 300-block of Water Street contains a compatible group of warehouses that are more distinguished architecturally than those in the preceding block. They offer various solutions to the problem of composing a 'tall' building. Here, white spandrels, bases, capitals, mouldings, and a prominent cornice interrupt the basic verticality of the red brick piers.

18
MARTIN AND ROBERTSON WAREHOUSE
313 Water Street
W.T. Dalton, c. 1899

Richardsonian Romanesque is the term used to describe the style of this warehouse and its two neighbours to the west. American architect Henry Hobson Richardson developed a popular style that featured round arches, heavy massing, and the use of rough-hewn stone and strong brickwork. The style spread west to Vancouver from Winnipeg – whence architect Dalton came – and north from Seattle.

19
HUDSON HOUSE
321 Water Street
W.T. Dalton, c. 1897

For more than sixty years the Hudson's Bay Company occupied this 5-storey warehouse, once one of the tallest buildings in Vancouver. Within the high arches the intermediate floors appear as spandrel beams; this arch-and-spandrel motif is a characteristic of the Richardsonian Romanesque style. The fine brickwork is complemented by rusticated stone trim. Twin pointed parapets top the façade.

20
GREENSHIELDS BUILDING
341 Water Street
1901

Robust rusticated stone piers at street level and carved capitals depicting heads of early Vancouver's different ethnic groups set in fanciful interlaced backgrounds enliven the façade of this warehouse for dry goods merchants Greenshields and Company. Thin vertical openings above the arch-and-spandrel windows are reminiscent of Richardson's influential Marshall Field Wholesale Store in Chicago (1885-7).

21
342 Water Street
1899

The Romanesque entrance arch, with carved capitals and a grotesque keystone head, reflects the more eclectic aspect of Richardson's architecture. Above the doorway the arch is abandoned and the more progressive pier-and-spandrel motif introduced. Rough-surfaced rusticated stonework provides rich texture. The Cordova Street façade, which curves to accommodate the alley, is as interesting as the front.

22
THE LANDING
375 Water Street
W.T. Whiteway, begun 1905

At a time when Gastown merchants were being hard hit by recession, the McLean Group redeveloped this large warehouse (originally built for wholesale grocers Robert Kelly and Frank Burnett) as an upscale complex of shops, restaurants, and offices (by Soren Rasmussen 1988). A new window punched through the back wall opens up a view of the harbour and the North Shore mountains.

23
HOLLAND BLOCK
364 Water Street
1891 or 1896

The recurrent bay windows and tapered flatiron form make the Holland Block a distinctive western entrance to Gastown. The bay windows were derived from the buildings of San Francisco. The Queens Hotel was an early occupant of the building. BC Ironworks provided the block with its cast-iron piers; note the foundry marks at their bases.

24
HORNE BLOCK
311 West Cordova Street
N.S. Hoffar 1889

J.W. Horne, who made his fortune in Ontario business and Manitoba land speculation, arrived in Granville in 1885 and soon became the largest private landholder in the city. Horne's office block was early Vancouver's most exuberant venture into the Italianate style. The façade used to be topped by a balustrade, and an ornate tower once rose over the Juliet balcony at the apex.

25
MASONIC TEMPLE
301 West Cordova Street
N.S. Hoffar 1888

Captain James Van Bramer helped to erect this attractive building for the Masonic Grand Lodge. Van Bramer had made his name as the captain of the *Sea Foam*, the first steam ferry to cross Burrard Inlet (in 1868) as well as the first to sink when it exploded at the Brighton wharf. As with so many early buildings, the cornice deteriorated and was removed for safety.

26
ARLINGTON BLOCK
302 West Cordova Street
1887

By the early 1960s the Arlington Hotel, like many of its neighbours, had deteriorated badly and was forced to close. The revitalization of Gastown really began here when, in the mid-1960s, property owners in the area conducted a 'paint-up' campaign, instilling new life into the Arlington and surrounding buildings.

27
UNITEL BUILDING
175 West Cordova Street
Francis Donaldson 1968-9

CP's Marathon Realty, Woodward's, Simpsons-Sears, and Grosvenor Laing Investments intended, in the 1960s, to redevelop most of Gastown with a mammoth scheme called Project 200. The plan was subsequently scaled down in scope and the consortium disbanded. The Unitel Building (formerly the CP Telecommunications Centre), shown here, and Woodward's parking garage (130-60 Water Street) were the only projects completed in Gastown.

28
CAMBIE HOTEL
312 Cambie Street
Parr & Fee 1899
This building represents one of Parr & Fee's earlier attempts to develop a new commercial style. Parr had worked in Winnipeg, Fee studied in Minneapolis; both had been impressed by the progressive developments in nearby Chicago. The plain brick piers (originally unpainted) and cast-iron window units of the Cambie were a marked departure from then-current styles.

29
PANAMA BLOCK
305 Cambie Street
1913
The construction of the Panama Canal promised to make Vancouver an important world port serving Europe as well as the Orient. The Panama Block was named in anticipation of the event. Cambie Street marks the western edge of the original Granville townsite. The streets west of here, part of the CPR's District Lot 541 surveyed in 1885, are aligned in a different direction, creating oddly shaped lots.

30
313-25 Cambie Street
1889
The ground-floor façade is recessed behind cast-iron columns, and shops are reached by staircases bridging the open area below street level, a common feature of British streetscapes but unusual in Vancouver. The upper storeys feature somewhat awkward elongated brick arches spanning pairs of windows and integrated into the brickwork.

31
STADIUM INN
340 Cambie Street
1896
This ruggedly textured brick and stone building was long known as the Commercial Hotel; the name used to appear on a pointed gable at the top. The original entrance to the hotel is now occupied by a beer parlour, and the new entry is through what was until recently the tiny Rose Bros. barber shop, probably the smallest building in the city.

32
COOK BLOCK
101-9 West Cordova Street
c. 1900
These three buildings, now orphaned on the corner by the oppressive mass of Woodward's overpass above Cordova Street and the huge parking garage, are all that remain of a block that once boasted the elegant Savoy Restaurant, Vancouver's first excursion into gourmet dining. The bow window of 109 West Cordova Street is particularly attractive.

33
76 West Cordova Street
R. MacKay Fripp, c. 1890
This is one of the few surviving buildings in Vancouver designed by talented architect R. MacKay Fripp. Born and trained in England, Fripp reached Vancouver in 1888 via Australia and New Zealand. The rough granite cornice balustrade is an outstanding feature of this building with its eclectic mix of robust stone and brickwork with classical detailing.

34
STANLEY HOTEL
21 West Cordova Street
1907

The Stanley and its neighbour, the New Fountain Hotel, were renovated in 1971 (by Henriquez & Todd) in an innovative project that combined commercial activity with the city's first privately developed rent-controlled housing. A passageway was cut through the hotel, opening onto heritage, award-winning Blood Alley Square, which in turn leads to Gaoler's Mews and to Water and Carrall streets.

35
LONSDALE BLOCK
8-28 West Cordova Street
N.S. Hoffar 1889

Two of Vancouver's leading businessmen, Thomas Dunn, a merchant and alderman, and Jonathan Miller, the city's first constable and postmaster, built this imposing building as the Dunn-Miller Block. Renamed the Lonsdale Block (A.H. Lonsdale purchased the block during the Klondike era), the long, unified façade recalls the terraced buildings of Georgian England. Twin roof pediments and pedimented windows impart a classical flavour.

36
BOULDER HOTEL
1 West Cordova Street
R. MacKay Fripp 1890

The Boulder Hotel is as robust as its name. Plain rectangular windows set into unadorned masonry walls were an unusual feature for the time, but they, and the rusticated stonework, give the building a muscular simplicity. The third storey, added about a decade later, blends successfully with the original structure.

Ho-Ho Chop Suey's

dazzling 1940s neon sign

Sun Ah Hotel

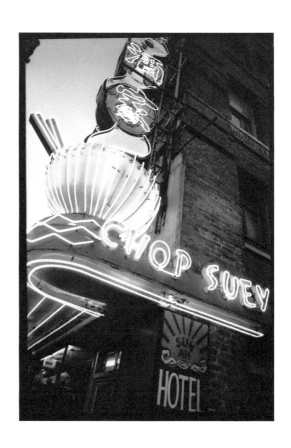

Area Two **CHINATOWN AND STRATHCONA**

G OLD fever lured many Chinese to British Columbia from San Francisco and Hong Kong during the Cariboo gold rush of 1858. They worked as miners and camp followers in the gold fields and shantytowns, but a Chinese merchant class grew, initially in Victoria, as the province developed. Vancouver's Chinatown developed in the 1880s when over 10,000 Chinese were imported to help build the CPR through the Rocky Mountains. Chinese based in Vancouver worked as cooks in hotels, mills, and logging camps, and ran laundries, import businesses, and fruit and vegetable farms. Less savoury were the opium dens in Chinatown's red-light district around Shanghai Alley.

The Chinese were not wholly welcomed by the province that benefited from their labour. The white population came to see the Chinese as competition, and in 1887 and 1907 the city was rocked by anti-oriental riots (also directed at local Japanese). But despite a federal head tax on Chinese immigrants and an immigration ban between 1923 and 1947 which dislocated families, the Chinese community grew and prospered.

The most serious threat to Chinatown came in 1967 when a free-

way was planned to bisect the area. This would have destroyed much of Chinatown's distinctive architecture and its urban flavour. Vociferous protest stopped the freeway, which would also have bulldozed much of neighbouring Gastown. Chinatown and Gastown were designated provincial historic districts and both areas have since been subjected to periodic 'improvement' projects of a well-intentioned but touristy nature. However, competition from the suburbs where most Chinese Canadians now live, combined with high property taxes which drain the small businesses that give Chinatown its character, threaten the district's future health.

Community well-being is also of concern in Strathcona directly to the east. Strathcona, named after Lord Strathcona, the Scottish-born director of the CPR, grew after Hastings Mill was opened at the foot of Dunlevy Street in 1865. It was the city's first residential district, but, after the railway arrived, financial and political influence moved with the city's new (largely eastern) social élite who settled on CPR property being opened up in the West End. Mill, cannery, and dock workers,

left: *Pender Street's façades are as varied and idiosyncratic as the shops below.*

right: *Strathcona's streetscapes retain their turn-of-the-century appearance.*

mostly of British stock, stayed on to be joined by continental European immigrants (the local school was multicultural long before the federal government enshrined the idea). Scandinavians, Germans, Ukrainians, Jews, Portuguese, and Italians settled in but moved on as their lot improved. Strathcona's ethnic mix today still includes Euro-Canadians but they are outnumbered by Chinese, Vietnamese, and Latin Americans.

The dead hand of urban renewal hung over the area in the 1960s poised to obliterate the run-down neighbourhood and all of its charming early architecture. Local opposition forced the planners to change their minds in favour of sprucing the area up, a process which continues today. However, social problems overflowing from the adjoining Downtown Eastside are persistent. Paradoxically, these problems have so far prevented an even greater threat to Strathcona's stability – gentrification.

37
CHINESE CULTURAL CENTRE
50 East Pender Street
James K.M. Cheng; Romses, Kwan
& Associates 1981
This significant building declares the Chinese community's role in BC history. The north-south axis, central entrance, inner courtyard, and covered second-floor walkways reflect traditional Chinese typology. The concrete post-and-beam structure's arcaded streetscape is embellished with a traditional gateway, made in China, and erected after display at Expo '86.

38
DR. SUN YAT-SEN CLASSICAL
CHINESE GARDEN
578 Carrall Street
Joe Wai 1986
This is the only full-size classical Chinese garden outside China, and the result of local initiative, diplomacy, and craftsmanship. The design recreates a scholar's retreat of the Ming period (1368-1644) and is based on examples in Suzhou. Artisans from that city built the tranquil garden and its exquisite pavilions using traditional techniques and materials.

39
CHINESE FREEMASONS
BUILDING
1 West Pender Street
c. 1901
In this blend of East and West, the Pender Street elevation sports the recessed balconies common in Chinatown and in coastal cities on the South China Sea from where the style is derived, while on Carrall Street the façade is solidly European. Note the 'cheater storey' here and on the nearby 1902 *Chinese Times* Building (the floor space was not taxed) between the first and second floors.

40
SAM KEE BUILDING
8 West Pender Street
1913

An infuriated owner, businessman Sam Kee, built this, the 'Thinnest Building in the World,' after Pender Street was widened leaving his property only six feet wide. Basement areaways, illuminated by sidewalk glass blocks, and second-floor bay windows ingeniously increase the floor space and luminosity. The building was restored (Soren Rasmussen 1986-7) for owner Jack Chow.

41
WING SANG BUILDING
51-69 East Pender Street
1889, 1902

A typical Chinatown building with a varied mix of tenants (there used to be an opium factory in the alley), this is otherwise unremarkable until you notice the original 1889 Wing Sang façade, the oldest building in Chinatown, swallowed by the 1902 addition. The older façade has the added curiosity of a door to nowhere on the second floor.

42
88 East Pender Street
E. Lee 1982

This well-mannered contemporary work is sensitively scaled to the existing streetscape by reference to the local tradition of recessed balconies. The rooftop pediment is a postmodern cliché but is used in correct classical fashion to accentuate the façade's symmetry. The exposed concrete column is a forceful contrast to the superfluous brick cladding.

43
SUN AH HOTEL
100 East Pender Street
Perky, White & Cockrill 1911

The hotel was once patronized by seasonal workers with jobs out of town but now, like other Chinatown tenements, its upper floors are occupied mainly by elderly Chinese. On the ground floor, Ho-Ho Chop Suey, one of the district's older restaurants, advertises itself with a dazzling 4-storey 1940s neon sign complete with steaming noodle bowl, chopsticks, and chubby typography.

44
CHINESE BENEVOLENT ASSOCIATION
108 East Pender Street
1909

Rusticated stone piers, lacy ironwork, and Cantonese signs in the recessed balconies animate this façade, one of the earliest examples of the Chinatown style. Chinese clan and benevolent societies provided social services and support for this immigrant community once beleaguered by racism and isolated, except as a source of cheap labour, from the rest of society.

45
MON KEANG SCHOOL
123 East Pender Street
J.A. Radford 1921

A rumour of classicism, picked up from the Lee Building next door (46), brings formality to the streetscape. Built by Wong's Benevolent Association as a clan office and Chinese school and broadly colonial in style, the building is infiltrated by Chinatown idiosyncrasies, including a lovely piece of stained glass chinoiserie above the main entrance.

46
LEE BUILDING
129-31 East Pender Street
1907

Similar in scale and style to the later Mon Keang School (45), the Lee Building has been completely rebuilt (by Henriquez & Todd 1973) behind the original, now free-standing, façade which acts as a screen through which access to a charming courtyard is gained. Shops and offices adapt to the established urban collage which gives the area its human scale and spicy air.

47
CHIN WING CHUN SOCIETY
160 East Pender Street
R.A. McKenzie 1925

Chinese recessed balcony treatment on the second and third storeys is given clumsy but likable pretension by the curved and triangular top floor, classical columns, and tiled, wainscotted entrance and doorway details on this unusually tall Chinatown façade.

48
BANK OF MONTREAL
178 East Pender Street
Birmingham & Wood 1971

This playful essay successfully edits the vertically framed, recessed balconies of its older neighbours. Subtle detailing, a Chinese tiled roof, and ornamental terracotta dragons soften the stark concrete structure. Postmodern, before the style was identified, it is more adventurous than the bank's new branch, which hides behind a dull heritage façade.

49
CANADIAN IMPERIAL BANK OF COMMERCE
501 Main Street
V.D. Horsburgh 1915

A stupendous, if delinquent, beaux-arts bank whose façade is framed by two pairs of banded Doric columns. These are of a monumental French order, but the composition is more ponderous than anything in the Paris of the day. Note the beautifully cut and letter-spaced period typography on the etched brass nameplates on the column plinths.

50
BC ELECTRIC RAILWAY SUBSTATION
700 Main Street
McCarter & Nairne 1945

This brick-faced concrete hulk seems haunted by the great industrial buildings of the 19th century. Its predecessor's elaborate, usually Italianate, decoration is here replaced by a heavy-duty moderne style. Two art deco doorways, with chevron and swash mouldings, and panels flashing with flames and bolts of lightning, energize the building's pilastered façade. Variegated brickwork adds pleasing texture to the design.

51
KUOMINTANG BUILDING
296 East Pender Street
W.E. Sproat 1920

The Kuomintang (Chinese Nationalist party) built their western Canadian headquarters here. Sproat, a Scottish architect, played safe with his unexpected client and designed the building in well-proven, turn-of-the-century commercial style. The delicate concrete piers and arches (formerly with recessed balconies) are reminiscent of 19th-century cast-iron buildings.

52
McLEAN PARK HOUSING SCHEME
Central Mortgage & Housing Corporation 1962-3, 1968-70

Local protest prevented all of Strathcona from being turned into an imitation of this arid utopia bounded by Keefer, Gore, Union, and Jackson streets. All the 1960s planning clichés are here, if less brutally deployed than elsewhere: separation of people from traffic (and amenities), walkways, bleak open spaces, point towers, and low-rise maisonettes.

53
451 East Pender Street
c. 1889

This Queen Anne style home, one of the oldest houses in the city, is characteristic of turn-of-the-century Strathcona. Restored in 1991, it is composed with bay windows, a balustraded porch and upper balcony, and conspicuous and enjoyable gingerbread gable ornament. The owner received a City of Vancouver Heritage Award in 1992 for the restoration.

54
JACKSON GARDEN
503 East Pender Street
H. Hou 1983

The street façades of this diminutive, inward-looking housing development might have been more assertive if two storeys taller, although the interior courtyards are expressively modelled, brick-faced, and pleasingly toy-town in scale, giving the impression of a little village in Holland or Scandinavia.

55
ST. FRANCIS XAVIER CHINESE PARISH CHURCH
431 Princess Street
J.G. Price 1910

Strathcona's changing, but consistently immigrant, character is evident in the successive congregations which have worshipped in this fine Gothic revival church which now serves the Chinese-Canadian Catholic community. Formerly it was St. Mary's Ukrainian Greek Catholic Church, St. Steven's Greek Catholic Church, and the First Swedish Evangelical Lutheran Church.

56
LORD STRATHCONA SCHOOL
592 East Pender Street
Thomas Hooper 1891

A potpourri of styles reflects the school's history. The oldest public school in the city, it was founded in 1865 as the Hastings Mill community school in a small clapboard building with fifteen pupils. The Keefer Street building (illustrated) dates from 1897. Remnants of the 1891 building's English brick and Scottish granite were incorporated into the Pender Street primary building. Later additions are by William Blackmore (1897) and C.L. Morgan (1913-27).

57
JACKSON APARTMENTS
660 Jackson Street
E.E. Blackmore 1910

This typical West Coast 3-storey walk-up is built in pattern-book Italianate style. Similar buildings can still be found elsewhere in the city, notably in the West End and Mount Pleasant. This is one of the most attractive with its confident cornice, corner oriel windows, and sociable corner grocery store. Note the verandahed row houses (1908) across the lane.

58
814-22 Jackson Street
1907
The gables, bay windows, and vertical emphasis expressed by the individual homes within the row of this Queen Anne style terrace recall the late-Victorian brick terraces of London and Toronto as much as the wooden row housing of 1880s San Francisco. The Queen Anne style is repeated on the adjacent house at the Union Street corner.

59
602 Keefer Street
c. 1902
A faceted entrance topped with a Victorian witch's hat turret, gables, and delicate gingerbread trim lend this whimsical Queen Anne home picturesque prominence on its corner setting. The house was once the home of a former headmaster of Lord Strathcona School.

60
630 Princess Street
c. 1902
Offset porch, gables, bay windows, and jigsaw trim maintain the original form of this early Edwardian home, although the original colour scheme, vividly over-painted, is anyone's guess. Few houses of this type were architect-designed. Most were assembled by local builders who would use pattern-book sources to model, for example, the lovely gingerbread decoration seen here.

61
ALEXANDER COURT
700 East Pender Street
1921
Originally built as the Sons of Israel Synagogue, this Romanesque revival building has been converted into condominiums (by Spaceworks Architects 1987) for Jacques Khouri, who also rehabilitated the Manhattan Apartments (178). It is a good example of the 'adaptive reuse' of a heritage building by which the exterior is preserved as a front for a completely rebuilt interior. Note the original dome, which has been reinstated above the internal courtyard.

62
730 Hawks Avenue
c. 1908
Originally a hostel for working men, and inventively transformed as row-house dwellings (Peter Auxier 1975), this building now has a small-scale village atmosphere accentuated by brightly painted balconies, picket fences, front doors, and pocket-size gardens which face the street, encouraging activity and neighbourly behaviour.

63
820 Union Street
Courtyard Group 1989
This postmodern design, handled with sophistication, shows that it is not necessary to copy the past in order to stay on speaking terms with older neighbours. The curved pediment and projecting window refer to the new home's turn-of-the-century milieu, but they do so on their own terms while still being receptive to the local scale.

64

**HOLY TRINITY RUSSIAN
ORTHODOX CHURCH
710 Campbell Avenue
Alexander Kiziun 1940**

In winter this building looks like a scene from *Dr. Zhivago*. Onion-domed churches are common on the prairies, where most Ukrainian immigrants settled before the First World War. This rare Vancouver example was built by the local priest who, despite the date, remained true to memory and distant, traditional form.

65

**500 Hawks Avenue
Walter Scott (builder) 1900**

This historic streetscape blushes with a fetching row of turn-of-the-century houses which have been restored (1986-7) (the two at either end of the row were built to replace the originals) as a communal project by the new owners. Note the similar unrestored row on the 400-block of Heatley and the three BC Mills houses (1903) at Nos. 507, 515, & 521 Hawks Avenue.

66

**LESYA UKRAINKA HOUSING
827 East Pender Street
Joe Wai 1987**

This apartment development strives to fit into the neighbourhood while proclaiming its own identity with a gaudy, gabled street frontage reminiscent of the decorative wooden vernacular of Russia and the Ukraine.

67
SEYMOUR SCHOOL
1130 Keefer Street
E.A. Whitehead 1900
Distinguished by a Second Empire roof, this is the oldest wooden school building in the city. The adjacent 1907 brick building (by W.T. Whiteway) is also of some interest. A standard school board design of the period, it is almost identical to Lord Roberts School in the West End (251).

68
ASTORIA HOTEL
769 East Hastings Street
Braunton & Leibert 1914
Originally the R.A. Wallace Building, this blowsy piece of Edwardian classicism is accented with pediments, paired pilasters, and deeply recessed bays handled with cheery confidence rather than expertise, but strong enough to withstand the fairground vulgarity of the hotel's 3-storey sign, later added.

69
UNITED GRAIN GROWERS
North foot of Vernon Drive
Barnett-McQueen Construction
1924
This structure was built to store prairie grain for export. Its design is strictly utilitarian, but look at its stirring scale. If you stumbled across this concrete hulk in the desert you might think you had found the monumental wreckage of a lost civilization. Grouped en masse, the sculptural ranks of cylinders also appear as a poetic vision of modernism's 'form follows function' dictum.

70
BC SUGAR WAREHOUSE
123 Rogers Street
1902

B.T. Rogers established Canada's first sugar refinery here in 1890 and later built two of the city's finest mansions (247 & 377). The industrial complex has several impressive buildings erected as the company expanded. The oldest is the 1902 Refined Sugar Warehouse, a spectacular brick building reminiscent of the best British industrial architecture of the 19th century.

71
BALLANTYNE PIER
North foot of Heatly Street
1921-3

Port buildings, like Victorian railway stations, were often built as gateways to cities or imperial trade routes. Ballantyne Pier, with its concrete quoins and arches imitating stonework, is no exception. Four functional storage sheds are each embellished with a colossal façade styled in the muscular, industrial classicism recalling the 19th century. All four façades may not survive proposed upgrading.

72
AMERICAN CAN COMPANY
611 Alexander Street
C.G. Preis 1925

This reinforced concrete factory shows the structural honesty and economy of expression of 19th-century engineers and their influence on modern architecture. The vigorous moderne external massing and atrium interior space (converted à la mode as designer showrooms, by Bruno Freschi 1988) contrast with the added external elevator pylon whose steel and glass recall the pioneering 19th-century engineering tradition.

73
DERA HOUSING CO-OPERATIVE
638 Alexander Street
Davidson & Yuen 1985

Modular façade and angled, tiled balconies bring a cubist dimension to this building. With an inner garden courtyard and relatively high density, it is a model of good urban design. The exposed structural concrete outwardly reflects the American Can Building (72) across the street (which the Downtown Eastside Residents Association had hoped to acquire) but is more mannered than its apparent mentor.

74
FLYING ANGEL SEAMEN'S CLUB
50 Dunlevy Street
1905

Formerly the head office of the historic Hastings Mill (356), this is now a seamen's mission. Originally built as a showhouse by the BC Mills, Timber & Trading Company to show off their methods of prefabrication, it is one of the company's more elaborate offerings, with Queen Anne dormer windows and a columned wrap-around verandah.

75
CANADIAN FISHING COMPANY
North foot of Gore Street
c. 1910

This is a survivor from the days when numerous fish processing and packing plants operated on Burrard Inlet and the Fraser River. It is a picturesque, vernacular building of a type once common to canneries on the coast all the way to Alaska, and a reminder of the continuing importance of the fishing industry to the provincial economy.

76

EMPIRE STEVEDORING
395 Railway Street
Watson & Blackadder 1941

The moderne style, more familiarly and exuberantly employed on cinemas and apartment buildings, is here elegant and restrained. The building is further distinguished and given authentic period flavour by the company's name set in bas-relief, contemporary lettering. Note the mainly Edwardian warehouse streetscape which this building terminates.

77

NEW WORLD HOTEL
396 Powell Street
Townsend & Townsend 1912-13

This was first known as the Tamura Building after the Japanese businessman who erected it. Restored in 1991, the building's rusting metalwork cornice and unorthodox corner Corinthian columns were repaired and recast in fibreglass. Architect Robert Lemon suggested the period colour scheme after taking samples from the original metalwork.

78

ST. JAMES ANGLICAN CHURCH
303 East Cordova Street
Adrian Gilbert Scott 1935-7

This is a tour de force – a bizarre neo-Gothic basilica suffused from the inside with Byzantine gloom. The English architect, a member of the Gilbert Scott architectural dynasty, had designed a cathedral in Cairo before this commission. Mediterranean, North African, and even Hollywood influences (there's a touch of beau geste here) show in the massive concrete walls and cool interior.

79
ST. JAMES CHURCH CLERGY HOUSE
303 East Cordova Street
Sharp & Thompson 1927
Gables, tile inserts, wide eaves, and roughcast wall surfaces found in the English arts and crafts and garden city vocabulary bring a polite, somewhat artificial charm to this attractive work. Note St. Lukes's home for the poor and aged (1924) next door on Cordova Street and the manse (1925) on Gore Street, both by Sharp & Thompson.

80
FIREHALL ARTS CENTRE
280 East Cordova Street
W.T. Whiteway 1905
Built as the headquarters of the Vancouver Fire Department and suitably imposing, this large fire station has been adapted as a theatre and arts centre (rebuilt 1976, by Roger Hughes). The building's decorative terracotta capitals and Renaissance arched bays (from where the fire engines once emerged) have been retained. Note the Georgian revival former Coroner's Court (by A.J. Bird 1932) next door, now the Vancouver Police Museum.

81
SALVATION ARMY TEMPLE
301 East Hastings Street
Mercer & Mercer 1949
This moderne building is more evocative of Hollywood than hymns and brass bands but is not without a messianic quality (the style, in more severe form, was favoured by totalitarian regimes between the wars). Here the characteristic assertive vertical and horizontal massing seems, given the date, passé and benign. Note the Orange Hall (by J. Gillott 1907) at 341 Gore Street with its Richardsonian entrance.

82

EMPRESS HOTEL
235 East Hastings Street
F.N. Bender 1912-13

This dowager long ago lost whatever prestige her name may have conferred, although a trace of Edwardian confidence and courtesy seems to remain (the bar sign announces a 'ladies' entrance). The hotel, its eight storeys piled up on a narrow lot, is in dramatic contrast to the other buildings on the block.

83

OVALTINE CAFE
251 East Hastings Street
c. 1942

The 200-block of East Hastings is one of many on the Downtown Eastside where jostling period façades and antique signs enliven the streetscape. There is a wooden gold rush façade at No. 239 which wouldn't look out of place in Barkerville. And, in a 1912 building (A.J. Bird), there's the Ovaltine Café – a paradise for those with retro taste and a love of formica and the louche vernacular of neon signs.

84

PROVINCIAL COURT BUILDING
222 Main Street
Harrison, Plavsic & Kiss 1972-4

Imposing piers and concrete walls, now softened by ivy on Cordova Street, reinterpret the columned pomp and ceremony of classical courthouse design with contemporary dignity. The fusion of Le Corbusier and brutalist influence is hardly subtle but does express authority and confidence in the rule of law. In this respect the building is very Greek, very classical.

Old signs and faded façades

preserve East Hastings Street's

traditional character.

Blue Eagle Café

Area Three   **DOWNTOWN EAST**

T WO distinct districts on Hastings Street, east and west of Victory Square, are included in this area: the old city centre at Hastings and Main and the grid planned by the CPR (commemorated on a bronze bas-relief attached to the former Canadian Imperial Bank at the southwest corner of Hastings and Hamilton streets) which marks the edge of today's city centre. In 1885, 'in the silent solitude of the primeval forest,' as the plaque puts it, Lauchlan Alexander Hamilton, the CPR Land Commissioner, 'drove a wooden stake in the earth and commenced to measure an empty land into the streets of Vancouver.'

Hamilton's system of east-west streets and avenues with Granville Street as its axis continued south across False Creek and formed the basis for future street layout as the city grew and expanded. Hamilton plotted the location of the CPR's station, offices, piers, and the Hotel Vancouver, effectively guaranteeing a westward shift in development from the existing Granville townsite (Gastown) to land granted to the CPR by the federal government. The odd angles of Court House (now Victory) Square, especially evident at the Dominion Building's dramatic

corner, indicate where Hamilton's grid abutted the Granville townsite.

Hamilton was elected to the city's first council in 1886 where he continued his planning activities by lobbying (against the interests of the CPR) for the creation of Stanley Park. In the same year, the land he had surveyed was cleared in preparation for development of the CPR's land holdings which stretched west from Cambie to Burrard Street and from Burrard Inlet to False Creek; an even larger CPR tract lay south of the creek, a part of which was later cleared to make way for Shaughnessy Heights.

Land sales in the new downtown took off with the arrival of the railway in 1886. Banks erected branch and regional head offices on the CPR land, and Hastings Street became the city's main thoroughfare. Construction of the Carnegie Library in 1903, next door to city hall on Main Street, maintained East Hastings Street's vitality until well into the Edwardian era. But the construction of grand, neoclassical banks on Granville Street, the General Post Office, and a new CPR station continued the westward movement of power and influence.

left: *The monumental Ionic colonnade of the old Canadian Pacific Railway Station.*

right: *Beatty Street's superb range of Edwardian warehouses is punctuated by the Second Empire dome of the Sun Tower.*

West Hastings Street has maintained its stature, but East Hastings has gradually declined – several blocks are now the city's Skid Road. The recent closure of Woodward's department store, like that of the BC Electric interurban station in the late 1950s, was a heavy blow. But agencies, such as the Downtown Eastside Residents Association, are struggling to overcome the area's problems, while endeavouring to preserve the invigorating urbanism and architectural heritage in the area. Victory Square, for example, is one of the finest Edwardian public spaces in Canada.

Encouragingly, the dense urban qualities of Downtown East have influenced the International Village, a mixed-use project being built on former railway land east of the Sun Tower, which will bring new residents and businesses into the area. There is concern, though, that development will displace those who already live in the area and that the city's heritage policy (which encourages, rather than ensures, preservation and re-use) may be inadequate to deal with future investment in the district.

85
BANK OF MONTREAL
390 Main Street
Honeyman & Curtis 1929-30

This sepulchral, miniature 'temple bank,' completed at about the same time as the Marine Building (171), marks the swan song of the neoclassical style. Proof of the banking establishment's incorrigible architectural conservatism and, to be more generous, of its desire to project tradition and security is demonstrated here by a columned entrance with pedimented doorway, topped by the bank's sculptural heraldry.

86
ROYAL BANK OF CANADA
400 Main Street
H.C. Stone 1910

A formal Ionic colonnade and an over-dressed cornice waltz along the façade of this Edwardian baroque bank which looks as if it should have been ten storeys taller. Hastings and Main streets were once the focus of the old city centre, but the area began to decline as business power and influence began to move westward around the time this branch was built.

87
ROYAL BANK EXTENSION
400 Main Street
Donald Matsuba 1976

This impeccable postmodern addition to the 1910 heritage original (86) respects its forebear's scale and fenestration but emphatically states that the times and architecture have changed. The new structure refers to the original's Italian mannerism with a vernacular classicism that is expressed with grace and simplicity.

88

CARNEGIE CENTRE
401 Main Street
G.W. Grant 1902-3

Scottish-American steel magnate Andrew
Carnegie funded this former library, now
a community centre (Downs/Archam-
bault 1980), designed in Romanesque/
Second Empire style. Redolent of high-
minded Victorian philanthropy, it is now,
paradoxically, the flagship of Skid Road.
Inside, in marble decrepitude, stained
glass portraits of Shakespeare, Burns,
and Walter Scott greet the city's poor
and disenfranchised.

89

REGENT HOTEL
160 East Hastings Street
1913

This late 19th-century Chicago style
building shows, in its arched vertical
pier-and-spandrel rhythm, the influence,
if not the sophistication, of the great
American architect Louis Henry Sullivan.
It is effective, nevertheless, as part of the
Downtown Eastside's varied early 1900s
streetscape.

90

McDONOUGH HALL
100 East Hastings Street
1888

One of the oldest buildings in Vancouver, this was constructed at a time when
the city was little more than a collection
of Wild West false-fronts, boardwalks,
and waterlogged streets. Note the unusual corner with its prominent bay and
cornice. The St. Andrews and Caledo-
nian Society built this property and held
meetings and, on at least one occasion, a
masked ball upstairs.

91
COTTON BUILDING
20 East Hastings Street
H.A. Hodgson 1911

This unremarkable Edwardian building is given salty presence by its main occupant, The Only Seafoods Fish and Oyster Café (1924), a diner that is as worth savouring as the area's faded architecture. The interior, previously the Vancouver Oyster Saloon, with its tiles, pressed tin ceiling, and counter-style seating is announced from the street by a superb neon sign.

92
TELLIER TOWER
16 East Hastings Street
W.T. Whiteway 1910-11

Completely refurbished as a housing co-op in 1989 by the Downtown Eastside Residents Association (DERA), this is a shining example of community-based urban regeneration and heritage preservation. Originally the Holden Building, built by local business baron William Holden, it served as city hall from 1929-36. It was renamed, ironically, after Gerald Tellier, a seaman and trade unionist.

93
PENNSYLVANIA HOTEL
412 Carrall Street
W.T. Whiteway 1906

Built originally as the Woods Hotel, this building's San Francisco style façade is composed in a rippling sequence of 4-storey oriel windows, strongly faceted at the corner (originally turreted). The building's overall scale and rhythm demonstrate exemplary turn-of-the-century urbanism. For years a Skid Road hotel, it is now managed by DERA which has restored some of its former respectability.

94

BC ELECTRIC RAILWAY COMPANY BUILDING
425 Carrall Street
Somervell & Putnam 1911-12

BC Electric once operated the most extensive interurban system in Canada from this building which served as a head office and tram depot (the tracks ran into the building from Hastings Street). Its stature is proclaimed in beaux-arts style, originally to have had a Parisian mansard roof and more sculptural decoration than finally applied. Note the traditional lobby behind three magnificent iron gates.

95

MERCHANTS' BANK
1 West Hastings Street
Somervell & Putnam 1912-13

Cast window frames, Corinthian capitals, entablature and frieze, pilasters, and heavy cornice – all resolutely neoclassical but now faded in grandeur – conceal a steel frame designed to support an even taller building. The façade was angled to accommodate the CPR spur line which ran from Burrard Inlet to False Creek before the Dunsmuir Tunnel (now used by SkyTrain) was opened in 1931.

96

ARMY & NAVY STORE
27 West Hastings Street
1908

Exposed steelwork, glazed mezzanine, and a wall of glass (originally topped by a graceful cornice) gave this building a precocious modernism which can still be sensed despite subsequent superficial alteration. Built for British importers Frederick Buscombe & Company, it was an exceptional building for its day. If restored, it would become one of the city's most outstanding buildings.

97
WOODWARD'S DEPARTMENT STORE
101 West Hastings Street
begun 1908

Charles Woodward opened a shop at the northeast corner of Main and Georgia in 1892, founding one of the largest retail chains in western Canada and establishing a Vancouver institution (the rooftop sign, a miniature Eiffel Tower, is a local landmark). The oldest building on the present 1903 site dates from 1908 (Hastings and Abbott). The store closed in early 1993 and this historic building's future is uncertain.

98
SHELLY BUILDING
119 West Pender Street
H.L. Stevens & Company 1911

This standard Edwardian office block with a middling, marble lobby sings out from the chorus line its contribution to the streetscape. It helps make the turn from Beatty Street to Pender particularly harmonious and influenced the scale of the neighbouring Pendera (99).

99
PENDERA
133 West Pender Street
Davidson & Yuen 1990

This exemplary inner-city housing block, developed by the indefatigable DERA, is an alternative to the tall, isolated towers that characterize much contemporary development. It is an instructive example, in neo-Edwardian warehouse style, of efficient high-density land use conforming to the existing urban fabric. One could argue, however, for a more modernist façade.

100
SUN TOWER
100 West Pender Street
W.T. Whiteway 1911-12

Publisher Louis D. Taylor wrote himself into the history books with this colossal structure which succeeded the Dominion Building (110) as the tallest in the British Empire. 'There is no limit to the possibilities of this city,' he once declared as mayor, bringing, what now seems, a Citizen Kane ring to his story and the look of his building – the free press symbolized in architecture. Note the rather risqué caryatids (by Charles Marega) which support the cornice.

101
BEATTY BUILDING
540 Beatty Street
Somervell & Putnam 1911

One of several warehouses which give this Beatty Street block a monumental and unified urban quality, the Beatty Building represents a departure from the usual beaux-arts style of the architects. The building has the stout Victorian character one finds in the textile mills of northern England and the dockland warehouses of Liverpool, a city whose repute, at the time, Vancouver aspired to.

102
550 Beatty Street
Bruno Freschi, c. 1980

This is a robust, brick-faced infill block with loft-style apartments above ground-floor commercial space, whose bulky elevation manages to avoid being mere pastiche. The building is in keeping with its Edwardian neighbours but also demonstrates its own quiet originality.

103
BEATTY STREET DRILL HALL
620 Beatty Street
1899-1901

The Department of Public Works had no hesitation in choosing an appropriate style when they planned this turn-of-the-century drill hall. They built a medieval fortress complete with battlements, turrets, and 3-foot-thick brick and granite walls. The rugged, semicircular turrets flanking the entrance are effectively composed and once faced a parade-ground across the street.

104
DEL MAR HOTEL
555 Hamilton Street
c. 1910

A collision between old and new resulted when BC Hydro began to demolish properties on the block to make way for their new tower (105). The owner of the Del Mar (which provides affordable accommodation for local residents) placed social conscience before business sense and refused to sell, forcing BC Hydro to reconsider the position but, unfortunately, not the appearance of the tower.

105
BC HYDRO BUILDING
333 Dunsmuir Street
Musson Cattell Mackey Partnership
1991-2

The overweight, dated postmodernism of this structure fails to match the stature of its predecessor (133). A mid-rise, high-density project might have been a more appropriate response to the site which borders the Victory Square historic district. The building does represent a significant eastward shift in development back towards the old city centre.

106

THE CENOTAPH
Victory Square
G.L.T. Sharp 1924

This 3- rather than 4-sided granite obelisk is designed to reflect the shape of the park where it stands. The sword, laurel and poppy wreaths, helmets, and Roman typography recall legions down the ages and here, specifically, Canadians who served their King and country in two world wars. The square was formerly Court House Square after the domed courthouse (1888) which once stood here.

107

PROVINCE BUILDING
198 West Hastings Street
A.A. Cox 1908-9

Vancouver's version of Fleet Street was once located by Victory Square. The *Daily Province* and the *Vancouver Sun* were once published within a block of each other. Both buildings survive but the streets seem listless compared to the days of eager reporters, speedy delivery vans, and the blowsy, Edwardian neoclassicism which the buildings share.

108

RALPH BLOCK
126 West Hastings Street
Parr & Fee 1899

Partly built with iron but less impressive than full-blown examples in New York or Glasgow, this building represents an unusual local use of the material. Wholesaler William Ralph had worked building bridges for the CPR and was familiar with iron structures. A 1992 DERA proposal to refurbish the façade and those adjacent as a screen for a new residential building suggested how this historic area might be revived.

109
FLACK BLOCK
163 West Hastings Street
William Blackmore 1899

Owner Thomas Flack struck it rich in the Klondike and expressed his good fortune with this rumbustious Richardsonian Romanesque block. A superb, ornately carved, round-arched entrance and a cornice parapet have long since been removed, but enough remains of the rusticated façade to warrant complete restoration. Note the Ormidale Block (by G.W. Grant 1900), directly east.

110
DOMINION BUILDING
207 West Hastings Street
J.S. Helyer & Son 1908-10

This extraordinary building was, for a short time, the tallest in the British Empire. It turns the Hastings/Cambie corner with Parisian élan. The mansard roof wouldn't look out of place on Haussmann's boulevards. Lavish terracotta decor topped by a scalloped cornice rise from a main entrance detailed with Adamesque ornament and dominated by two titanic Roman columns. The original stairs enhance the interior.

111
ROGERS BLOCK
301 West Hastings Street
c. 1898

This nicely textured Klondike-era commercial building mixes red brick with rusticated granite string-courses and lintels. There is a pleasing cornice effected with bracketed brickwork and a stone string-course. Irregular fenestration and unusually generous glazing is achieved by the use of cast-iron mullions. Note the buildings to the west which continue the historic streetscape.

112
CANADIAN IMPERIAL BANK OF COMMERCE
300 West Hastings Street
Dominion Construction 1959

Banks abandoned their trusted neoclassicism after the war and paddled towards the shores of modernism and the international style (this building is a modest example). This is also the site, commemorated by a fine bas-relief plaque, where Lauchlan Hamilton, the CPR's land commissioner, began to survey the land for the future city in 1885.

113
VANCOUVER COMMUNITY COLLEGE
250 West Pender Street
Sharp & Thompson, Berwick, Pratt 1948-9

Modern architecture was introduced to the city centre in this international style building erected by the school board. Strip windows and stucco spandrels are set off against red brick walls producing the clean lines characteristic of the style. Some Bauhaus-inspired elegance remains, although the building has been altered over the years.

114
LYRIC THEATRE
300 West Pender Street
1906

This tough building in Richardsonian Romanesque style stoutly maintains its wounded pride despite being somewhat assaulted by alteration. It terminates a streetscape of enchanting period serendipity, with small businesses as varied as the architecture lining both sides of the 300-block of West Pender Street.

115
BC PERMANENT LOAN COMPANY
330 West Pender Street
Hooper & Watkins 1907

Coupled columns, generally associated with beaux-arts fashion, support the pediment on the portico of this exquisite miniature example of the style. The federal Bank of Canada occupied the building from 1935 to 1966, installing a machine-gun emplacement to defend an enlarged vault. The pièce de résistance, by the Bloomfield firm, is the banking hall's Tiffany style stained-glass dome.

116
WEST PENDER BUILDING
402 West Pender Street
H.S. Griffith 1912

This aristocratic office block has a virtually intact period interior: marble lobby, wainscotted corridors, varnished wood office doors with frosted glass and painted company names, and a brass Royal Mail box fed by chutes from all floors. The pilastered banking hall once boasted the 'safest armoured steel vaults in the West' until they were penetrated in a daring heist in 1977.

117
VICTORIA APARTMENTS
514 Homer Street
c. 1898

This 3-storey Victorian tenement is drawn from earlier, more elaborate San Francisco examples, whose influence drifted north during the late 19th century. Note the typical use of oriel windows but with an unusual and sociable Dutch stoop.

118
NIAGARA HOTEL
435 West Pender Street
Grant & Henderson 1912

The scene here is straight out of a 1940s film noir, animated by the Niagara's spectacular neon sign, with its tumbling waters cascading down the hotel's façade onto rocks and neon pine trees. The sign, now a classic of its kind, was designed by Laurence Hanson of Neon Products, Canada, in the early 1950s, at a time when the city's cinemas, dance halls, and old hotels glowed like Broadway.

119
LUMBERMEN'S BUILDING
509 Richards Street
J.P. Matheson & Son 1911

The Northwest Trust Company built this handsome brick and terracotta commercial block which rises with some dignity from the surrounding parking lots and faded hotels. Cornice detail, powerful vertical emphasis, and the particularly fine Renaissance terracotta-tiled ground-floor exterior, where the Lumbermen's Bank was located, distinguish this design.

120
HOLY ROSARY CATHEDRAL
646 Richards Street
T.E. Julian & H.J. Williams 1899-1900

This was once a lone sentinel on the skyline like the medieval Gothic cathedrals of France from which it takes its cue. The site was chosen by the priest because the tallest tree in the city stood here, although it was promptly cut down to make way for the church. Steeples, buttresses, a vaulted interior, a carillon, and a rose window are fine features. Note the adjoining manse, also in sandstone.

121
SEYMOUR BUILDING
525 Seymour Street
Somervell & Putnam 1912
Reinforced concrete and skyscraper-Gothic soar to ten storeys with gusto and assurance. The entire elevation is covered with glazed terracotta, a popular façade treatment in Seattle where the architects had their main office. Lovely top-floor tracery and lower niches are reserved for sculptural figures but have never been filled. Note the architects' neoclassical London Building (1912) at 628 West Pender.

122
EXCHANGE BUILDING
568 Seymour Street
1913
This was remodelled as a record store (by Baker, McGarva, Hart 1989) in brash but vigorous contrast to the restored terracotta façade. The neoclassical cladding was made in England, probably by Doulton of Lambeth, London. Doulton was known at the time for its architectural terracotta. The second Hotel Vancouver at Georgia and Granville (1913, demolished 1948) boasted much Doulton tilework, which included moose and buffalo heads.

123
CANADA PERMANENT BUILDING
432 Richards Street
J.S.D. Taylor 1911-12
This neoclassical gem is alive with eclectic invention: semicircular balconies, decorative ironwork, Doric pilasters, and a flat pediment capped with beavers and a castellated tower (the company motif). Eccentric doorway treatment, splayed at the base in ancient Egyptian fashion, rises through a small pediment to enclose a clerestory window. The superb marble interior with carved woodwork repeats the exterior style.

124

BANK OF BRITISH COLUMBIA
490 West Hastings Street
T.C. Sorby 1889

There are traces of past elegance here, but this Italianate former bank head office has fallen on hard times. The cornice balustrade and the angled corner entrance have been lost and only two of the ground-floor arches remain on this historic building, which should be restored. The 400-block of West Hastings is rich in old façades. No. 404, the Royal Bank of Canada (1903) was the city's first 'temple bank.'

125

SPENCER'S DEPARTMENT STORE
515 West Hastings Street
McCarter & Nairne 1928

David Spencer emigrated from Wales in 1862 and set up shop in Victoria before moving to Vancouver in 1906. His store became a household name in the city, remembered long after Eaton's took it over in 1948. This jazzy 1928 building was converted to offices as part of the Harbour Centre (126) and, in 1990 (by Aitken Wreglesworth Associates), as Simon Fraser University's downtown campus.

126

HARBOUR CENTRE
555 West Hastings Street
Webb, Zerafa, Menkes, Housden & Partners; Eng & Wright 1974-7

This is a typical 1970s status symbol – a shopping mall and office tower topped, to attract tourist business, with a flying saucer-shaped, revolving restaurant. The confusing complex is saved from total banality by the exterior elevators which whiz up and down the façade like a scene from the film *Metropolis*.

127
STANDARD BUILDING
510 West Hastings Street
Russell, Babcock & Rice 1914
More impressive for its size – 15 storeys of steel frame clad with brick and terracotta – than architectural quality, this neoclassical block sprouts top-floor neo-Gothic ornament (a fashionable addition showing the influence of New York's Woolworth Building of 1913). The lobby, a florid piece of Edwardiana, has been restored and extended in a pleasing spatial sequence to an adjacent expresso bar.

128
INNES-THOMPSON BUILDING
518 West Hastings Street
C.O. Wickenden 1889
The importance of this design is as much historic as architectural. Built next door to the original CPR offices, it was one of the first permanent buildings on the land granted to and promoted by the railway, and marks the westward development from Gastown. A rare survivor, it displays the unsophisticated charm of its time – a combination of frontier vigour and metropolitan pretension.

129
TORONTO DOMINION BANK
580 West Hastings Street
Somervell & Putnam 1919-20
A late-flowering neoclassical design, Edwardian in spirit and Greco-Roman in inspiration, this bank's fine cornice detail and playful top-floor arched windows contrast with the Ionic solidity below. The banking hall façades are skilfully articulated within the overall composition. Currently derelict, this building should be preserved, perhaps as a ruin, like the lost classical world, whence its style came.

130

PRICE WATERHOUSE CENTRE
601 West Hastings Street
Tudor & Walters 1983-4

This looks like a 1950s science fiction space station, unfortunately, not sent into orbit. It attempts to upstage the nearby CPR Station but it is not exceptional enough to justify this conceit. Aluminium and mirror glass seem inappropriate given the surrounding urban context. The clumsy gazeboed plaza, a frigid public space, replaced the Richardsonian Romanesque 1888 Empire Building.

131

ANGEL OF VICTORY
Old CPR Station
601 West Cordova Street
Coeur de Lion MacCarthy 1922

This poignant and unexpected encounter with the past – a bronze angel spiriting a soldier heavenwards from the trenches of the First World War – was commissioned by the CPR to commemorate the company's war dead. The design, by an Ottawa sculptor, was cast at Mount Vernon, New York, with identical castings for the stations at Winnipeg and Montreal.

132

OLD CANADIAN PACIFIC
RAILWAY STATION
601 West Cordova Street
Barott, Blackader & Webster
1912-14

A potent national symbol, this building expresses the corporate pride and decorative taste of the time. Formerly the terminus of the CPR, restored for transit, office, and retail use (by Hawthorn/Mansfield/Towers 1976-8), its neoclassicism is dignified by an Ionic colonnade and a superb luminous booking hall decorated with salon-style landscapes of the scenery through which the trains passed.

Vancouver's purest and best

example of modernism

Dal Grauer Substation

Area Four   **DOWNTOWN WEST**

TODAY'S central business district, concentrated on either side of Burrard Street from Robson Street north to Burrard Inlet, was a residential area at the turn of the century. Christ Church Cathedral, the former parish church, and a handful of apartment buildings and houses are the only reminders of this period.

During the Edwardian boom years, commercial development on Hastings Street and up Granville overflowed to the west in an un-planned fashion. Lots on the land surveyed by the CPR had been sold off individually for residential use between Granville and Burrard streets, and while many buildings subsequently erected in the Edwardian era were styled in neoclassical and beaux-arts fashion, this influence did not extend to formal town planning (historically, the focus of the city's development has been haphazard and subject to a frontier mentality and boom and bust economics). The Winch Building (1909), the first commercial building west of Granville, and the General Post Office (1905-10) (both now part of the Sinclair Centre) form a balanced streetscape. But the Crédit Foncier Building and the Vancouver Club,

completed just before the outbreak of the First World War, are more typical of the city's urban diversity.

Construction of the Marine Building in 1929-30 firmly established the central business district's architectural profile on Burrard Street. Tenants of this remarkable art deco edifice included the principal grain, shipping, marine insurance, and merchantile companies in the ambitious port city. Vancouver, a key transit point on the CPR's 'all red route' between Great Britain and her colonies in the Far East, had expanded even more when grain and lumber shipments started going through the Panama Canal in 1913.

The Burrard Street corridor today displays a representative collection of city architecture – from Gothic revival Christ Church Cathedral and the châteauesque Hotel Vancouver to the modernist BC Hydro Building and the postmodern Cathedral Place. One of the finest buildings here is the 1957 Vancouver Public Library, a modernist work which is currently the subject of a heated heritage debate. Plans for a new library, a postmodern design (by Moshe Safdie and Downs/Archam-

left: *Exuberant and exquisitely crafted art deco ornament on the Marine Building (entrance detail)*

right: *One of several column and pediment arrangements on the neoclassical Provincial Court House (now the Vancouver Art Gallery)*

bault) stunned citizens when they were unveiled in 1992 (the building bears more than a passing resemblance to the Colosseum in Rome). The new building is to be partly funded by the disposal of the old library, even though the latter is one of several postwar buildings to have been 'A'-listed in a 1992 update to the city's heritage inventory.

Historic Granville Street has fared less well than Burrard Street over the years. The Pacific Centre mall sucked shoppers underground in the 1970s. Robson Street, by comparison, has retained its effervescence, cars and all. However, Robson Square, a 1970s attempt to create a planned civic public space, is somehow lost in foliage and informality, designed to reflect the city's natural setting. Current redevelopment on Coal Harbour by Canadian Pacific's Marathon Realty also seems as influenced by the city's setting as it is by traditional urban qualities. The main feature of the plan will be a waterfront promenade from which one can look not at the city but at the sea and the North Shore mountains beyond.

133
BC HYDRO BUILDING
970 Burrard Street
Thompson, Berwick & Pratt 1955-7
This beacon of modernism is still luminous with the optimism of its time. The porcelain and glass curtain wall acts as a semi-transparent screen for the lozenge-shaped floors cantilevered out from a central core (as in the contemporary Pirelli Building in Milan). Abstract mosaics by B.C. Binning and other period details are well preserved in this, the first postwar work to receive city heritage designation.

134
DAL GRAUER SUBSTATION
970 Burrard Street
Sharp & Thompson, Berwick, Pratt 1953-4
Here an expressive steel and glass curtain wall is composed with the dynamic geometry of a Mondrian painting. Classical in its poise and central bay, it brilliantly reveals, especially at night, its electrical inner workings and social purpose, true to the modernist 'form follows function' style. BC Hydro, which operates the substation, evolved from the old BC Electric Railway Company (94).

135
PROVINCIAL LAW COURTS
800 Smithe Street
Arthur Erickson Architects 1973-9
A 'not proven' verdict still hangs over this controversial, structurally adventurous building, conceived to demystify and make accessible the traditional portals of justice. It succeeds in this respect with its space-framed, galleried public concourse, but it is compromised by tradition and closed courtrooms into which the public space dissolves.

136
ROBSON SQUARE
800-block Robson Street
Arthur Erickson Architects;
Cornelia Oberlander (landscape
architect) 1972-9

A cross between Frank Lloyd Wright and the hanging gardens of Babylon might best describe this, at times confusing, but imaginatively planned, layered public space. It manages both to inspire and infuriate with tantalizing, occasionally formal views glimpsed through a foliage of relentless informality – the genius loci being West Coast rather than truly urban.

137
VANCOUVER ART GALLERY
750 Hornby Street
F.M. Rattenbury 1906-12

Rattenbury's talent flowered in the romantic eclecticism of the Empress Hotel and the Parliament Buildings in Victoria rather than in the heavy neoclassicism of this work, built as the Provincial Court House (rehabilitated 1979-82, by Arthur Erickson Architects). Nevertheless, the building boasts impressive porticos and a fine rotunda revived as an internal focus in the art gallery conversion. Note the Tuscan columned drinking well (by Charles Marega 1912) on Hornby Street.

138
COURT HOUSE LIONS
North portico, Vancouver Art
Gallery
John Bruce 1910

This imperious pair was carved by a Scottish sculptor who modelled them on those by Sir Edwin Landseer sited in Trafalgar Square, London, in 1867. Today the lions guard a purposeless portico, previously the entrance to the courthouse, but sealed when the building was rebuilt as the Vancouver Art Gallery.

139
HOTEL GEORGIA
801 West Georgia Street
R.T. Garrow & John Graham, Sr.
1926-7

A late Georgian revival design, the hotel, with its enjoyably pseudo-classical wood-panelled lobby and well-preserved, polite exterior detail, has a sentimental appeal and townscape charm which outweigh its modest architectural merits. Liverpool-born Graham was, in his day, one of Seattle's most prominent architects.

140
TORONTO DOMINION TOWER
700 West Georgia Street
Cesar Pelli 1969-71

This steel-framed, curtain-walled tower of considerable power and austerity is echoed across Georgia Street by the IBM Building (1973-5), a smaller companion, both part of Pacific Centre, Phase 1 (by Victor Gruen & Associates; McCarter, Nairne & Partners). Together they remain the city's purest demonstration of the Miesian 'less is more' philosophy. A less elegant part of the project is Eaton's department store (1970-2), also by the same consortium.

141
PACIFIC CENTRE, PHASE 2
700 West Georgia Street
Zeidler Roberts Partnership 1988-9

This inoffensive rather than inspired addition to the Pacific Centre attempts to humanize and bring street credibility to the 1973 underground mall with a bridge across Dunsmuir Street, skylit galleria and office tower, an entrance rotunda at Georgia and Howe, and heritage bric-à-brac pasted to the Granville Street façade, north of Dunsmuir.

142

SCOTIA TOWER
650 West Georgia Street
Webb, Zerafa, Menkes, Housden &
Partners 1974-7

Judging by the list of names, it took the combined talents of several architects to design this building, the focus of the Vancouver Centre mall. But many hands did not make light work here. The resulting scheme, an appalling blot on the streetscape, destroyed the Birks Building, one of the city's finest Edwardian commercial blocks.

143

BIRKS CLOCK
Southeast corner of Georgia &
Granville
c. 1900

A fine example of decorative cast iron, manufactured by the Howard Company, Boston, around the turn of the century, this is the only reminder of the famous Birks Building, a 1912-13 Somervell & Putnam design built for Montreal jewellers Henry Birks & Sons, demolished in 1974. The clock originally stood outside Trorey Jewellers at Hastings and Granville.

144

VANCOUVER BLOCK
736 Granville Street
Parr & Fee 1910-12

This building looks like a wedding cake with an icing of terracotta cast to form caryatides and Greco-Roman ornament applied for no good reason other than flamboyant one-upmanship of questionable taste. At fourteen storeys, this engagingly boisterous building couldn't match the Sun Tower (100) as the tallest in the British Empire but it may have had the Dominion's biggest clock.

145
HUDSON'S BAY COMPANY
Georgia & Granville
Burke, Horwood & White 1913,
1926

A gigantic emporium built in the exuberant neoclassical style which became a Hudson's Bay trademark (similar HBC department stores can be found in Calgary and Winnipeg, while an almost identical twin stands in Victoria), this design employs lavish terracotta, especially on the palatial colonnades, to camouflage the utilitarian pier-and-spandrel elevations.

146
GENERAL POST OFFICE
349 West Georgia Street
McCarter, Nairne & Partners;
Department of Public Works 1953-8

The GPO was designed when public institutions in Britain and the Commonwealth saw themselves in the vanguard of postwar progress, and it was built accordingly – on a grand scale. The exterior style alludes to the influential 1951 Royal Festival Hall, London. Inside are factory-like distribution spaces and a fine modernist postal hall. An underground train once linked the GPO to the CPR station.

147
CANADIAN BROADCASTING CORPORATION
700 Hamilton Street
Thompson, Berwick, Pratt &
Partners 1973-5

This broadcasting centre is built, seemingly, to withstand a revolution. The concrete bunker architecture (to reach the studios you descend below ground), generally pilloried by staff and public alike, is nonetheless powerfully composed (by Paul Merrick) with huge conduits (to ventilate the studios) exposed in a high-tech manner to avoid the transmission of vibrations.

148
CAVELTI BUILDING
555 West Georgia Street
Townley & Matheson 1928

Formerly the Randall Building, this modest art deco block's Gothic terracotta heraldry was repeated by the architects on the grander Stock Exchange at 475 Howe Street. City planners and jeweller Tony Cavelti negotiated heritage designation and a density bonus that financially facilitated rehabilitation (Blewett, Dodd, Ching, Lee 1991) by allowing an additional storey to be set back on the roof.

149
BC ELECTRIC SHOWROOM
600 Granville Street
Hodgson & Simmons; McCarter & Nairne 1928

This neoclassical, somewhat Spanish, curiosity is overlaid with stagy, part-burlesque, part-grand, opera decor. Unusual cast-bronze window frames rise impressively through two storeys decorated with delightful arabesques which, with the projecting window bays, seem to echo with faint sounds of flamenco tunes.

150
CANADIAN IMPERIAL BANK OF COMMERCE
586 Granville Street
McCarter & Nairne 1958

An attentively designed modernist bank built to traditional urban scale, the CIBC evokes the spirit of its age with a stunning Venetian mosaic mural by B.C. Binning, celebrating provincial industries, crafts, and natural resources. 'From a banking seaport of the old world to a financial and shipping centre of the new' declared the Imperial Bank, aware of the Renaissance roots of corporate patronage.

151
BANK OF MONTREAL
580 Granville Street
Somervell & Putnam 1916; K.G.
Rea 1924-5

Originally the Merchants' Bank, this building was enlarged with the addition of a Corinthian-columned entrance and three bays up Granville Street. The bank's coat-of-arms, displaying its head-dressed, feathered Indians, was also added above the cornice. The building's subtle but extensive neoclassical detail is well preserved and, remarkably, the period banking hall is largely unaltered.

152
ROGERS BUILDING
470 Granville Street
Gould & Champney 1911-12

Seattle architects Gould & Champney designed this extravagant terracotta palazzo, clad with terracotta tiles that completely cover both street façades with a neoclassical veneer. The impressive granite-columned entrance once led to the building's most extraordinary feature – a tiled, mirrored, basement barbershop that looked like a room from the Palace of Versailles.

153
TORONTO DOMINION BANK
499 Granville Street
McCarter & Nairne 1948-9

This forceful, modernist composition is given horizontal emphasis by finned sunshades or *bris soleil*. It is one of the earliest buildings to have awakened a dormant downtown to the possibilities of progressive postwar architecture, although this is not evident in the rather conservative mural of George Vancouver inside.

154

CANADIAN IMPERIAL BANK OF COMMERCE
640 West Hastings Street
Darling & Pearson 1906-8

Massive fluted Ionic columns, deep-set eaves gallery, a heavy cornice, and rigid adherence to classical precepts combine in granite façades to create an impression of stability and unimpeachable authority in this classic 'temple bank' by the Toronto firm which specialized in this type of building and in this style.

155

ROYAL BANK BUILDING
675 West Hastings Street
S.G. Davenport 1929-31

The Royal's Montreal-based chief architect envisioned the tallest and largest bank in Vancouver when he planned this half-built skyscraping palazzo. Enough remains of the neo-Romanesque design to show just how grand it would have been. One is tempted to open an account just to be able to regularly visit this stunning Florentine arcaded banking hall.

156

SINCLAIR CENTRE
757 West Hastings Street
Henriquez & Partners; Toby, Russell, Buckwell & Partners 1983-6

This exemplary project by Public Works Canada has modern offices and a bijou shopping arcade, intriguingly layered behind the restored façades of four heritage buildings. The unadorned contemporary construction of the arcade and galleria counterpoints the more delicate period notes struck by the older buildings' decorative details which are recycled throughout.

157
GENERAL POST OFFICE
Sinclair Centre
757 West Hastings Street
David Ewart; Department of Public
Works 1905-10

This wonderful beaux-arts building is the most imposing and convincing example of the style in the city. A particularly well-handled corner sequence rising through paired columns and curved pediments to a dome and cupola anchors the composition's rusticated arcades and colonnades. Note the Parisian mansard roof and delightful weather vane.

158
WINCH BUILDING
Sinclair Centre
757 West Hastings Street
Hooper & Watkins 1908-9

No expense was spared on this the first commercial building erected west of Granville Street. Business baron R.V. Winch (who pioneered the salmon-canning trade, built a mansion in the West End, and drove around the city in a 1910 Rolls Royce) spent much of his fortune on this Renaissance palazzo with its colonnaded top floor, ground-floor arcades, and tiled interior.

159
FEDERAL BUILDING
Sinclair Centre
757 West Hastings Street
McCarter & Nairne 1935-9

This extension to the General Post Office was designed, one senses, by a committee. Its spare, modern form is embellished with enough neoclassical and art deco decoration, fastidiously detailed, to have kept everyone happy. To the architects' credit, the building emerged with dignity and withstood some loss of symmetry during reconstruction. Note the adjoining Customs Examining Warehouse (1911-13).

160
GRANVILLE SQUARE
200 Granville Street
Francis Donaldson 1971-3
A stark but honest building, this was the only large structure to emerge from the abandoned Project 200 (see 27). At 32 storeys, it was tall enough to attract the harbour air traffic control tower to its roof. The rather bleak plaza below is humanized by an ironic piece of public art by Michael Phifer which is symbolic of forests, cities, and cultural totems.

161
WATERFRONT SKYTRAIN STATION
Swan Wooster; N.D. Lea 1986
Clean, functional, modern design is here employed in exemplary fashion married to the old CPR Station (132). The lesson that, if in doubt, keep it simple is amply demonstrated here (note the Howe Street entrance) and throughout the SkyTrain system where sensible signage, durable materials, and good design have established the transit system's identity and the perception, at least, of efficiency and reliability.

162
815 West Hastings Street
Eng & Wright 1975-6
This handsome, classically inspired, brick-faced building makes the effort to be friendly towards its older companions – particularly the Metropolitan Building (1912) directly to the west whose scale and dismantled cornice the newer building was designed to reflect. Ironically, the Metropolitan Building is threatened with demolition.

163
789 West Pender Street
Northwood & Chivers 1929;
McCarter, Nairne & Partners 1970
A marriage of convenience connects the Hall Building (1929) on Howe Street and the setback former Montreal Trust Building (1970) on West Pender. The relationship is mutually tolerant, even sympathetic, with the newer building's vertical piers responding to its elder's emphasis but without the latter's vigorous neo-Gothic personality. Raimund Littmann redesigned the interior (also 14 & 193) for Novam Development.

164
BC & YUKON CHAMBER OF MINES
840 West Hastings Street
J.C. Day 1927
The Chamber of Mines discovered this gem of a building in 1959, painted their claim in gold letters on the window, and mounted a huge relief map of the province's rumpled interior on the wall. The map was once shipped to London to interest investors in the mineral-rich terra incognita. The building, an odd but likable antique, was built for the Royal Financial Trust Company.

165
CEPERLEY ROUNSEFELL COMPANY BUILDING
846 West Hastings Street
Sharp & Thompson 1921
An exquisite Georgian revival façade, which wouldn't look out of place in London, is here marred by unsympathetic modern signage. The building complements the Vancouver Club across the street (167), by the same architects. The original full-height interior hall has long since been filled in.

166
CREDIT FONCIER BUILDING
850 West Hastings Street
Barrot, Blackader & Webster
1913-14

This superb neoclassical palazzo was clad with granite ashlar, concealing a reinforced concrete frame built for the Montreal-based Crédit Foncier Franco-Canadien. Twenty-six Corinthian columns (22 on the eaves gallery), a pilastered ground-floor arcade, and a richly detailed copper cornice combine in a composition of great distinction.

167
VANCOUVER CLUB
915 West Hastings Street
Sharp & Thompson 1912-14

London was the inspiration for this businessmen's club designed in Georgian revival style by immigrant English architects to emulate the aristocratic clubs of St. James. It is a convincing copy with a splendidly wood-panelled dining room and general ostentation redolent of establishment privilege in Britain's imperial heyday.

168
WATERFRONT CENTRE
900 Canada Place Way
200 Burrard Street
Musson Cattell Mackey Partnership
1990-2

A case of architectural (and planning) stage fright, the two dumpy, postmodern towers, clad with mannered, stepped fenestration, are a cautious clichéd response to a magnificent sea and mountain setting. The scheme is partly redeemed by a plaza (part of which, perversely, is below grade), the hotel tower's graceful curve, and the arcaded Cordova Street sidewalk.

169
CANADA PLACE
999 Canada Place
Zeidler Roberts Partnership; Musson Cattell Mackey Partnership; Downs/Archambault 1983-6

This impressive, decked, mega-project was built as the Canadian pavilion for Expo '86 on the site of Canadian Pacific's Pier BC, from which the famous Empress liners sailed to the Orient. Teflon-coated sails strung in high-tech fashion enclose an exhibition hall/conference centre, while the interior of the hotel superstructure boasts lofty public spaces.

170
DAON BUILDING
999 West Hastings Street
Musson Cattell Mackey Partnership 1980-1

This thoughtfully arranged tower was seemingly designed to play second fiddle to the Marine Building (171), which its reflective glass both illuminates and refracts, but is massed and angled to command its own corner. Public open space and leafy landscaping, favoured by planners (although not always a good idea), works well here despite the pocket plaza's poorly chosen slippery tiles.

171
MARINE BUILDING
355 Burrard Street
McCarter & Nairne 1929-30

This expressive art deco monument was conceived, as the architects put it, as 'a great marine rock rising from the sea, clinging with sea flora and fauna.' Skyscraper setbacks are awash with mesmerizing terracotta decoration symbolizing the city's seaborne trade and aquatic setting. Renovated in 1989 (by Paul Merrick), the building's arched, faceted entrance and vaulted foyer sequence is a tour de force of late 1920s decor.

172

UNIVERSITY CLUB
1021 West Hastings Street
Sharp & Thompson 1929

An engaging Spanish colonial revival essay, this building was designed by the
same architects as the Vancouver Club
(167) with which the University Club has
since merged. Originally built for the
Quadra Club, and for a time the headquarters of the local Royal Canadian Air
Force Reserve, it was bought by the
University Club in 1957.

173

OCEANIC PLAZA
1066 West Hastings Street
Charles Paine & Associates 1976-7

A stablemate of the Guinness Tower
(174) by the same architects and developers, the two buildings are linked by a
graceful pedestrian bridge. The classical
influence found on international style
buildings is seen here in the precision of
the Pender Street arcade, the Hastings
entrance, and in the fluted, columnar effect of the tower's vertical piers.

174

GUINNESS TOWER
1055 West Hastings Street
Charles Paine 1967-9

This exemplary international style building is composed with Miesian minimal-
ism, lightness, and clarity. The elegant
ground floor features a wonderful lobby
mural by Jordi Bonet which reworks the
Marine Building's decorative themes
with chaotic, aquatic objets trouvés
which counterpoint the tower's cool,
aloof presence.

175
PORTAL PARK
1000-block West Hastings Street
Pavelek & Associates 1987

A postmodern folly faintly reminiscent of Italian Renaissance garden pavilions (although somewhat heavy-handed by comparison), the park is effective as a formal public space for contemplation of the city's luminous natural setting. The car park between the CPR Station (132) and the Landing (22) would benefit from similar treatment.

176
BENTALL CENTRE
595 Burrard Street
Frank W. Musson & Associates
begun 1965

Concrete precast piping flowering in rooftop epaulettes softens the Miesian curtain walls of this development's four towers with an attenuated classicism characteristic of the new formalist style. The plaza fountain by George Tsutakawa, a 1960s Picasso-style piece, stands out from the generally ordinary public art in the city.

177
MacMILLAN BLOEDEL BUILDING
1075 West Georgia Street
Erickson/Massey; Francis Donaldson 1968-9

This magnificent building powerfully expresses forestry giant MacBlo's corporate personality and purpose, with 27 storeys of load-bearing, poured-in-place concrete taper (the wall thickness is a gradation of eight feet at the base to eight inches at the top) like colossal tree trunks. More correctly though, the allusions here are classical – Erickson has called it his 'Doric façade.'

178

MANHATTAN APARTMENTS
784 Thurlow Street
Parr & Fee 1908

The florid design of this building, with double-barrelled cornice brackets lushly carved with acanthus leaves, a pilastered, recessed entrance, and oriel windows, was highlighted by 1970s renovation by developer Jacques Khouri (see also 61) after residents saved the landmark from the wrecker's ball. The narrow courtyard and columned passage are pleasantly reminiscent of 19th-century arcades.

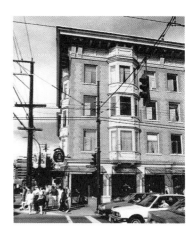

179

BURRARD BUILDING
1030 West Georgia Street
C.B.K. Van Norman & Associates 1955-6

This was the first large international style office building to be erected in Vancouver, although you wouldn't know it today. The building was literally stripped of its identity and integrity in a recent renovation project (by Musson Cattell Mackey Partnership 1988-90) which replaced the original curtain wall and open floors with mirror glass and enclosed interiors.

180

VANCOUVER PUBLIC LIBRARY
750 Burrard Street
Semmens & Simpson 1956-7

Built as the city's central library, this is the best of a diminishing number of highly regarded modernist buildings in Vancouver. Echoes of the Bauhaus and constructivism show in the library's creative use of space and brisk geometry. Planned construction of a new public library opposite the CBC Building makes the future of this significant building uncertain.

181
HOTEL VANCOUVER
900 West Georgia Street
Archibald & Schofield 1928-39

No Canadian city would be complete without a Franco-Scottish railway hotel. The Hotel Vancouver was built by the CNR, managed for a time by Hilton (who ripped out much of its stately interior), but has now been restored to its former glory by CP Hotels. French Renaissance detail and extraordinary medieval gargoyled whimsy cloak the exterior. The château roof is de rigueur. Note the superb bas-relief with a steamship and a train above the main entance.

182
CHRIST CHURCH CATHEDRAL
690 Burrard Street
C.O. Wickenden 1889-95

The oldest surviving church in Vancouver, this was built to serve a growing parish in the West End. Fine stained glass casts soft light in the interior which boasts a marvellous hammer-beam timber roof. A cathedral since 1929, it was saved after an early 1970s attempt to replace it with an office tower and underground sanctuary. Ironically, it has now lent its name to adjacent Cathedral Place.

183
PARK PLACE
666 Burrard Street
Musson Cattell Mackey Partnership 1984

A sunlit, verdant plaza complements this handsome, if slightly mannered, tower developed with the aid of a density transfer from neighbouring Christ Church Cathedral. Flush-fitted windows and the pale granite curtain wall react to light and weather conditions with a chameleon-like chicanery, cleverly diffusing the tower's otherwise portly appearance.

184
CATHEDRAL PLACE
925 West Georgia Street
Paul Merrick 1990-1

This elegant postmodern tower responds well to its setting with 1920s skyscraper massing recalling the preceding Georgia Medical/Dental Building which it, controversially, replaced. Coy retro details (griffins and roof from the Hotel Vancouver and nurses re-cast from the Medical/Dental Building), fitted to appease heritage advocates, but also the result of the architect's engaging whimsy, make it a building of its time and a future curiosity.

185
CANADIAN CRAFT MUSEUM
639 Hornby Street
Paul Merrick 1990-1

A reprise of Cathedral Place which it faces across a courtyard, this little building has a restrained interior (contrast with Cathedral Place's neo-Gothic lobby) displaying terracotta panels salvaged from the entrance of the Georgia Medical/Dental Building. Outside, in typical postmodern fashion, the façade plays with historical styles, including deco reliefs from the Georgia Building.

186
HONGKONG BANK OF CANADA
885 West Georgia Street
Webb Zerafa Menkes Housden Group 1984-6

The muscular massing of this postmodern bank evokes 1930s skyscraper design. The luminous atrium, though, is beautifully finished with polished stone surfaces. One of the city's more exciting public spaces, it is animated by sculptor Alan Storey's 'pendulum.' An apocryphal tale has it that a passerby saw the piece move and phoned the fire department thinking the building was about to collapse.

Sensitive warehouse

rehabilitation has preserved

Yaletown's streetscapes.

1000-block Hamilton Street

Area Five **DOWNTOWN SOUTH**

ALONG the south and east fringe of the downtown area lies a diverse and largely undeveloped area known as Downtown South. Its three principal parts are Yaletown, the Granville Street corridor, and the Expo Lands, all of which vary in origin and character.

Yaletown, the area formerly located around Drake Street, east of Granville, was developed in the late 19th century by the Canadian Pacific Railway. Houses and sheds came to Vancouver by flatcar from the CPR's former maintenance depot in Yale. New construction formed a 'company town' within municipal boundaries. A tunnel (now used by SkyTrain) linked the yards, in 1931, with the main line along Burrard Inlet. The Kitsilano Trestle (now dismantled) provided rail access across False Creek just east of the Burrard Bridge to the industries further south along the Fraser River.

Remnants of this community remain, notably, the Roundhouse, the only railway structure to survive. The social life of the area is recalled by the Yale Hotel and a handful of 1880s frame houses. Yaletown's proximity to the CPR freight yards encouraged the growth of a large commercial

distribution centre with imposing brick and concrete warehouses. After trucking challenged rail freight, many warehouses were rehabilitated as offices and lofts in a predictable, but healthy, process of gentrification.

The Granville Street corridor runs through the western edge of Yaletown from the city centre to the Granville Street Bridge. This commercial strip developed with one-storey retail stores interspersed with budget office buildings and rooming houses. Several fine theatres were built here as well, including the Orpheum and the Granville. North of Nelson, Granville Street was converted, in the 1970s, into a landscaped pedestrian-and-bus mall, with only limited success. The area's potential as a mixed-use, residential, commercial, and entertainment district and Granville Street's potential as the city's Champs-Elysées is so far unfulfilled.

East of Yaletown is a former industrial area which once reeked of smoke-belching mills and factories built mostly on filled land on the tidal flats of False Creek. The industries disappeared during the 1960s and 1970s. Cleared and augmented by more fill, the land along the

left: *The shape of things to come – 889 Homer Street's postmodernism reflects the changing nature of Downtown South.*

right: *Yaletown's warehouses were once plastered with company signs. The Pacific Milk sign, on the 1200-block Homer Street, is a rare survivor.*

Creek enjoyed fleeting glory as the site of Expo '86. The site was cleared after the fair, and only BC Place and Science World remain. A large portion of the Expo Lands is currently under development by Concord Pacific Developments, who bought the land (one-sixth of downtown) from the provincial government. Pacific Place is a mammoth project that will mix residential units with commercial and public space. A costly cleanup of contaminated soil began in 1992.

The area between downtown, the Expo Lands, and Yaletown (south of Robson and west of Homer) has been named 'Downtown South' by city planners. Their hope is to bring a cohesive West End style to a neighborhood better known for its nightclubs and light industry. High densities, tall buildings, and a mixture of residential and commercial uses slotted within the existing street grid are encouraged by new municipal zoning regulations. Developers have responded with several projects aimed at a variety of income levels, from assisted housing to luxury condominiums designed in a variety of styles.

187
CPR ENGINE NO. 374
Davie Street & Pacific Boulevard
Engine No. 374, built at the CPR shops in Montreal in 1886, pulled the first transcontinental passenger train into Vancouver in 1887. The historic locomotive, formerly displayed at Kitsilano Park, exhibited at Expo '86, and restored by a loyal band of volunteers, is now preserved with the Roundhouse and turntable.

188
CPR ROUNDHOUSE
Davie Street & Pacific Boulevard
CPR Engineering Department 1888
This unique industrial relic is a reminder of the city's growth as a Pacific railway terminus and of the CPR freight yards and workshops which, until the 1970s, covered the north shore of False Creek. Built to a standard CPR design, the building, with its impressive cedar-columned interior, is to become a community centre as part of the Pacific Place redevelopment.

189
YALETOWN HOUSE
1099 Cambie Street
Downs/Archambault 1984-5
With bay windows and sympathetic massing, this building acknowledges its turn-of-the-century setting in the Yaletown warehouse district. Designed as a senior citizens' home, the complex features rooftop gardens, an intimate enclosed courtyard, and a strongly modelled presence on Cambie Street.

190
YALETOWN BUILDING
1152 Mainland Street
1913

Heavily serifed railway-era numerals painted down the side of this brick façade echo the days when Yaletown warehouses were plastered with company signs. Former tenants here included the National Bag Company and the Canadian Naval Store, but there are no signs announcing that now. Today's names are discreetly posted inside the entrance, reflecting the district's gentrification.

191
MURCHIE'S TEA & COFFEE
1200 Homer Street
Thomas Hooper 1912

A stately 6-storey warehouse of traditional appearance but reinforced concrete construction, Murchie's Tea & Coffee Limited (established in 1894) now occupies the building and uses it as a head office as well as a warehouse. Murchie's added the slightly fussy decorative spandrel panels after they moved in 1985.

192
CANADIAN LINEN SUPPLY
1200 Richards Street
Townley & Matheson 1932

A vestige of the light industry rapidly being elbowed out of this area by residential development, this is a good example, still with its original chimney, of the 1930s penchant for dressing up industrial buildings in the fashionable moderne and art deco styles of the day. Clean lines and white painted concrete, here more classical than moderne, reflect the popular modernism of the time.

193
1090 Homer Street
c. 1910

This traditional brick warehouse reveals a robust early modernism on its rear façade. Massive cedar beams and columns, and brick firewalls inside, have been retained during seismic upgrading and stylish office/retail conversion by Novam Development (1992), one of the pioneers of Yaletown's renaissance. Video post-production and photography have replaced valve and lubricant services here.

194
YALETOWN CENTRE
1038-40 Hamilton Street
Thomas Hooper, c. 1910

Dentils, a brick bracketed cornice, and a parapet are attractive items retained on this warehouse, rehabilitated as offices (Stuart Howard Architects 1988) along with its neighbour (1912) to the south. The main entrance, in a pleasing piece of urban design, becomes a passage between Hamilton Street and the Mainland Street's former railway loading bays, the latter a typical Yaletown feature.

195
1014 Homer Street
Dominion Construction 1931

Fluted pilasters rise through the cornice to a moderne parapet which is the focus of this building, originally a General Motors office and renovated in 1986. Notable art deco ironwork on the ground floor is complemented by a Parisian-style butterfly canopy not unsympathetic to the original design but clearly post-modern in its effect.

196
889 Homer Street
Bing Thom 1991-2

This inventive, 27-storey postmodern residential tower is flanked by related, but smaller, commercial blocks. The composition's disparate elements – exposed, weathered concrete; quirky, faintly secessionist, steel canopies; symmetrical 1920s massing on the Homer Street elevation; modernism; and hints of classicism – coalesce with unexpected ease, even elegance.

197
857 Beatty Street
Thomas Hooper 1910

A plain, but rhythmic, brick façade, enlivened by the slope of the street, conceals a spacious, if spartan, interior built for Campbell Cold Storage but now converted (Mark Ostry 1988) from warehouse use to artist's ateliers. An old freight elevator, which creaks with elderly charm, serves all floors. A notable group of warehouse lane façades are at the rear.

198
BC PLACE STADIUM
777 Pacific Boulevard
Phillips, Barratt 1983

Stadiums can be designed with functional beauty, usually a combination of the engineering bravura and elegance encountered on suspension bridges and cable-stayed or free-form concrete structures. BC Place, despite its air-filled fabric roof, is not in this class and is included here more for its size than design merit. Note the Plaza of Nations and the BC Pavilion across Pacific, built for Expo '86.

199
TERRY FOX MEMORIAL
Beatty Street entrance to BC Place
Franklin Allen 1984
This postmodern triumphal arch is, aside from its worthy sentiment and effective punctuation at the end of Robson Street, very difficult to like. The mirrored image and typographic commemoration inside the arch is a thoughtful idea unfortunately overwhelmed by the monument's self-indulgent style.

200
COMMODORE BALLROOM
870 Granville Street
1929
Distiller George Reifel built this popular dance hall, apparently on a whim of his wife who thought that the old Hotel Vancouver (where Eaton's now stands) shouldn't be the city's only reputable night spot. Recent interior remodelling has left the Spanish colonial/art deco façade in its original condition.

201
ORPHEUM THEATRE
884 Granville Street
B. Marcus Priteca 1926-7
A beaux-arts façade on Granville Street gives no warning of the wonders inside the Orpheum. The auditorium is an amazing mélange of architectural styles and colour, happily saved by popular demand and civic pride when it was threatened with demolition in 1973 (and renovated in 1975-6 by Thompson, Berwick, Pratt & Partners). Priteca was the doyen of West Coast theatre designers, designing over sixty from San Diego to Alaska.

202
VOGUE THEATRE
924 Granville Street
Kaplan & Sprachman 1940-1

The architecture of early cinemas was based on the styles of the theatres and music halls which the cinemas mostly replaced. By the 1920s, however, movie theatre design had become a flamboyant expression of Hollywood and the world projected on the silver screen. The Vogue, with its huge sign and expressive modernistic exterior, is a more sombre essay in the style.

203
SOUND SPECTRUM
929 Granville Street
c. 1910

The Wilson and La Salle buildings have been combined in this example of adaptive re-use of heritage buildings (rehabilitated in 1989 by Perkins & Cheung). A new canopy and a boldly sculptural neon sign complement rather than imitate the heritage character which has been retained in structural form and façade detail.

204
1000-block Granville Street
Parr & Fee 1910-13

The Royal, Regal, Vogue, and Glenaird hotels (and others on blocks south) form a consistent, historic grouping on this dilapidated strip of Granville Street. The buildings are typical of architects Parr & Fee's bread-and-butter commercial work. Regular fenestration, heavily bracketed cornices, and glazed brick façades are characteristic features.

205
BANK OF NOVA SCOTIA
1196 Granville Street
Sharp & Thompson 1929
This is an unusual art deco bank branch, perfectly preserved by benign neglect (the area's general shabbiness seems to have discouraged interior or exterior changes to the design). Classical demeanour, delicate art deco details, and a faintly Egyptian air to the entrance, lend the building a good-humoured rather than pompous integrity.

206
YALE HOTEL
1300 Granville Street
N.S. Hoffar 1890
Originally known as the Colonial Hotel, this building was patronized by workers from the CPR yards and locomotive maintenance sheds bordering Yaletown. The hotel, still with rooms upstairs but 1950s scrolled neon lettering outside, is now a popular jazz bar. The mansard roof and dormer windows are uncommon features on the West Coast. The style is French provincial, via Quebec.

207
GEORGE LESLIE HOUSE
1380 Hornby Street
c. 1888
This delightful house is a rare survivor of old Yaletown. Enlivened by a 2-storey bay window, jigsaw balcony, and porch trim, the house was built by tradesman G.L. Leslie. Italian restaurateur Umberto Menghi took over the house in 1972, expanded into the shop next door, and then commissioned a stucco and tile extension (by Werner Forster 1976).

208

FALSE CREEK YACHT CLUB
1661 Granville Street
Bing Thom 1989-90
This shipshape, if not entirely graceful,
waterfront building seems about to set
sail. The nautical effect, achieved by high-
tech cables, masts, decks and hand rails,
and factory materials is not inappropriate, given its purpose and setting. It faces
Granville Island whose industrial vernacular the yacht club hails from across the
creek.

209

1000 BEACH AVENUE
1000-block Beach Avenue
Hulbert Group 1991-2
This extremely mannered, postmodern
high- and low-rise project, whose regur-
gitated constructivism, touches of Le
Corbusier, and docklands vernacular are
overlaid with a veneer of glitzy pretension (part of the tower's porte-cochère
is a swimming pool with a glazed bottom) is an effective part of a high-density
residential zone between the Granville
and Burrard bridges.

210

BURRARD STREET BRIDGE
J.R. Grant (engineer); Sharp &
Thompson 1930-2
The Burrard Bridge was designed with
two levels, one for cars and one for
trains, to supplement the old Granville
Bridge and to better serve the growing
West Side suburbs. Grant's steel structure was camouflaged at the behest of
the Public Art Commission (who also in-
sisted on a single deck) in the Spanish
colonial/art deco style fashionable at the
time.

West End towers jostle

for the best waterfront views.

English Bay

Area Six **THE WEST END**

IN 1859 the crew of the survey ship HMS *Plumper* found coal on the shore of Burrard Inlet near the foot of Bute Street. Coal Harbour was never mined but the discovery led three Englishmen to search for clay for brickmaking. In 1862 the 'Three Greenhorns' purchased the West End's 550 acres for around a dollar an acre. The brickmaking venture failed, although Coal Harbour did become an industrial zone of mills and boatyards. After trying to sell some of their land, the Greenhorns were persuaded to give a third of it to the CPR as part of the railway's land grant.

In 1887 the CPR began to develop its lands. Georgia Street, west of Burrard, became 'Blueblood Alley,' the choice residential enclave of Vancouver's moneyed élite. The city began buying waterfront property to allow public access to the shore (a policy still supported) and established Stanley Park. The park area, completely forested as the West End had been, had long been used by Natives (Deadman's Island was an Indian burial ground). In the 1850s the Royal Navy had occupied the park's peninsula for harbour defence. This prevented land speculation

and when the Dominion government gave the land to the city it was still semi-wild. The park, named and dedicated in 1889, has become one of the city's most valued assets. With its seawall walk, cricket pitch, floral displays, and occasional eccentric monuments, it retains an air of civilized leisure.

Change is more evident in the adjacent West End. After 1900, apartment buildings began to appear among the single-family homes. Commercial development was hastened, mainly along the streetcar lines on Davie, Denman, and Robson streets. Merchants and immigrants moved in as the well-to-do flitted to the CPR's newly developed Shaughnessy Heights. Robson Street became a little Europe, 'Robsonstrasse,' as it was known, only recently having assumed its chichi, designer air. Larger homes were converted to rooming houses and suites or demolished.

Even so, when the Sylvia Hotel was built in 1912, the West End was still a leafy suburb of mansions and modest homes. It wasn't until 1958 that the Sylvia lost its title as the tallest building in the area after a 1956

left: *An elaborate sequence of pediments blossoms above the verandah of Barclay Manor, one of the West End's surviving Edwardian homes.*

right: *Breezy, seaside postmodernism at the corner of Denman and West Georgia*

pro-development zoning change lifted a 1927 (the city's first) residential height restriction. The architectural free-for-all that followed gave the neighbourhood, one of the most densely populated and cosmopolitan districts in the country, its jungle of towers. The high density has promoted a healthy population mix and attendant services, bringing to the area European traditions of urban life.

Few of the modern buildings are of individual merit, but grouped en masse they do make a memorable forested skyline. Surprisingly, in the undergrowth and sediment below, many older buildings survive in layered reference to the community's past. Since the 1970s, zoning, traffic management, and heritage preservation have improved the West End's livability. However, the redevelopment of Coal Harbour by Canadian Pacific's Marathon Realty, now proceeding after a lengthy public process, and the Bayshore Gardens scheme at the Stanley Park end of Georgia Street promise further change.

211
FIRST BAPTIST CHURCH
969 Burrard Street
Burke, Horwood & White 1910-11
A parapeted and buttressed granite bell tower anchors this Gothic revival design to its corner site. The spacious sanctuary is fitted with a wooden coffered ceiling and balconies. Rough stonework contrasts with the ashlar on the grander St. Andrew's-Wesley across the street (212), with which the First Baptist Church forms a gateway to the West End.

212
ST. ANDREW'S-WESLEY UNITED CHURCH
1012 Nelson Street
Twizell & Twizell 1931-2
This resolute late Gothic revival building's concrete construction is concealed by a veneer of traditional stonework. The impressive, solemn interior is illuminated by superb stained glass, mainly by Morris & Company (England) and Gariel Loire (Chartres, France), and energetic modern glass by Lutz Haufschild (Canada) in the south transept.

213
ST. PAUL'S HOSPITAL
1081 Burrard Street
Robert F. Tegen 1912
The hospital was established in 1894 by the Sisters of Providence, a Catholic order founded in 1845. The first building was replaced by this brick and terracotta edifice designed in Italianate style reminiscent of 19th-century London. Balconies, Romanesque window arches, cornice detail, and a Tuscan belvedere are, unfortunately, overwhelmed by 1930s wings and extensions.

214
1100-block Comox Street
c. 1898
This late 19th-century West End street-scape, remarkable for its consistency and survival, shows how the area once looked: block after block of single-family houses animated by turrets, bay windows, classical columns, and gingerbread trim. Little remains of this early architecture – even the grander homes are almost extinct – making this streetscape an invaluable heritage resource.

215
NICHOLSON TOWER
1115 Nelson Street
Erickson/Massey 1968-9
In this federal and provincial government project for senior citizens, raw, shuttered concrete walls are moderated by elegant design, providing a contrast with the vast, dismal housing schemes elsewhere which have given social housing a bad name. Note 1230 and 1260 Nelson Street (1970) for a more mannered example of the architects' brutalist style.

216
THE CAPRI
1080 Barclay Street
c. 1955
European and Mediterranean in more than its name, this building shows, in its clean design, the influence of Le Corbusier and the European avant-garde of the 1920s. Horizontal strip windows cutaway at the corners, and the flat roof, glazed stairway, and supporting pilotis mark this building's stylistic origins.

217
1235 Nelson Street
c. 1931
Snappy, 1930s art deco-cum-neo-Gothic detailing enlivens this 3-storey walk-up. An identical twin stood next door until it was demolished in 1991. While the survivor gains stature by its sibling's demise, the loss to the streetscape is unfortunate.

218
1225 Barclay Street
Hywell, Jones 1988
This building looks like a 1930s ocean liner which has ploughed its way ashore. The sensuous curving façade recalls the moderne style of sixty years ago – an appropriate inspiration for a still progressive port city. It is the best individual building in a notable, modern, high-density grouping.

219
THE BEACONSFIELD
884 Bute Street
J.S.D. Taylor 1909
A handsome block of flats, this was one of the first apartment buildings to be erected in the West End. The building's notable features include two cavernous bays filled with wooden balconies with art nouveau balcony kingposts, and a Palladian window in the recessed entrance court.

220
BANFF APARTMENTS
1201 West Georgia Street
H.B. Watson 1909

This beautiful Italianate apartment block has a columned entrance on Georgia Street and façades alive with arches, Juliet balconies, and bowed oriel windows. The interior once contained a skylit gallery. The original plans show domes that were never built. The Banff's cornice line is continued by the equally fine Stadacona Apartments (1911) further down Bute Street.

221
MOORE BUILDING
626 Bute Street
McCarter, Nairne & Partners 1968

Designed by Blair MacDonald, this quiet building's refined composition manages to temper the normally overbearing brutalist style. The deeply recessed windows act as sun breaks in Le Corbusier's Mediterranean mode and are balanced on the elevation by the low, cavelike entrance through which the plaza paving seamlessly enters the foyer.

222
THE BANFFSHIRE
610 Jervis Street
Thornton & Jones 1911

This Georgian revival-cum-Jacobean block of flats has an air of 19th-century London about it. Oriel windows, patterned brickwork, Adamesque ornament, columned doorways, and its Scottish name lend the Banffshire a convincing aura of the fin-de-siècle bourgeois society exported throughout the British Empire.

223
EVERGREEN BUILDING
1285 West Pender Street
Arthur Erickson Architects 1978

This building successfully blends and reflects Vancouver's urban environment and wilderness setting. Its difficult triangular site has been expertly handled with stepbacks hung with greenery which fall away from the modernism of the cityside elevation. It gives the illusion of a corporate world that is relaxed and informal behind the suits and ties – very West Coast.

224
WESTCOAST ENERGY BUILDING
1333 West Georgia Street
Rhone & Iredale 1968-9

A magical building, this is as much a triumph of structural engineering as architecture. Engineer Bogue Babicki adopted the proven principles of the suspension bridge here by hanging the floors and curtain wall from steel cables draped over the top of the concrete service core. The stepped podium and framed views from the open ground floor add a surreal formality.

225
CROWN LIFE PLAZA
1500 West Georgia Street
Rhone & Iredale 1976-8

In this example of 'technological brutalism,' Miesian curtain walls coalesce with exposed concrete towers and pilotis, employed with gutsy sophistication (inspired by the work of James Stirling in the UK). The tower, watery plaza, and single-storey retail space are each expressed in a triangular plan, brilliantly arranged to make the most of mountain views and the sloping site.

226
ROBSON PUBLIC MARKET
1610 Robson Street
Romses, Kwan & Associates 1986

Ersatz Victorian, iron-and-glass, barrel-vaulted arcades became a shopping mall cliché in the 1980s. But this basically 19th-century structural style is versatile and can be used as more than just pastiche in the contemporary urban scene. Robson Market reworks the traditional market hall theme with just the right blend of workaday purpose and informal charm.

227
LORD STANLEY TOWER
1684 Alberni Street
Field, Hong & Associates 1979

The highly mannered brutalism of this building cleverly exploits the effects of hard sunlight and deep shadows. There are echoes of 1920s Russian constructivism in the cubist juxtapositioning of angular canopies, balconies, projecting fins, and the elevator shafts and chimneys which thrust through the roof with youthful vigour.

228
1888 Alberni Street
Spaceworks Architects 1990-1

Meretricious but inventive postmodernism animates this building, whose energetic curving façade and well-articulated elevations show more thought than the goofy party-hat turret suggests. The imaginative, bow-arched vehicle entrance reworks the porte-cochère theme. The tiled water garden and smooth, columned main entrance convey a soothing classical calm.

229
BAYSHORE HOTEL
1601 West Georgia Street
Douglas Simpson & Associates
1960-1; Reno Negrin & Associates
1969-70

The Bayshore, which stands on a former sawmill site, is a pleasant and fairly typical 1960s resort complex caught somewhere between the era of Elvis Presley Hawaii movies and the present day. It is a precursor of the redevelopment which will transform Coal Harbour from a waterfront of boatyards and railway tracks to a dense high-rise office and residential zone.

230
VANCOUVER ROWING CLUB
Stanley Park
J.W. Keagey 1911

The Vancouver Rowing Club was formed in 1886, the year the city was incorporated. The original boathouse, once moored at the foot of Burrard Street, was replaced by the present clubhouse designed in picturesque English Victorian style, convincing enough to look good on the River Thames. The pilings holding the rambling structure in place were rebuilt (by Keith Watson-Donald) in the 1980s.

231
ROBERT BURNS MEMORIAL
Stanley Park
1928

This copy of a 19th-century Burns statue in Ayr, Scotland, is cast from the original mould. The Vancouver Burns Fellowship Society erected this piece, a reminder of the traditionally strong Scottish connections in Canadian society. The same pensive bronze figure stands in Dominion Square, Montreal. Note the bas-relief poetic plaques attached to the granite plinth.

232
STANLEY PARK PAVILION
Stanley Park
Otto Moberg 1911

Stanley Park was never affected by imperial vistas and grandiose plans – although
there was a 1920s proposal (designed by
McCarter & Nairne) to erect a neoclas-
sical/art deco art gallery at Lost Lagoon.
The buildings in the park, like this tea-
room built in CPR Swiss chalet style – all
gables and rustic disorder – have a vernacular quality appropriate to the setting.

233
JAPANESE-CANADIAN WAR
MEMORIAL
Stanley Park
James Benzie 1932

Erected by the Japanese Association to
commemorate Japanese Canadians who
fought in the First World War, this
fluted, classical column topped by an oriental lantern symbolizes the two cultures and is a poignant memorial coloured, from today's perspective, by the
internment of Japanese Canadians during
the Second World War.

234
TOTEM POLES
East of Brockton Point cricket
ground

This is a striking, if historically inaccu-
rate, assemblage of totem poles. They
look authentic enough, but the poles
have significance to tribes further up the
coast (who would group them in linear
patterns facing the sea) rather than to
local clans. Stanley Park's poles are
tourist totems. Local dilettantes set
aside the site in 1912 intending to recre-
ate an 'Indian Village.'

235
LIONS GATE BRIDGE
**Palmer & Bow (architects);
Monsarrat & Pratley, Robinson &
Steinway (engineers) 1937-8**
Financed by the Guinness brewing family
to provide access to the British Properties and promoted as the 'largest suspension bridge in the British Empire,' the
bridge has since been surpassed by
longer and more graceful designs. Best
seen from the Stanley Park seawall, it
leaps dramatically from Prospect Point
but descends with a structural whimper
on the landward ramp on the North
Shore.

236
SOUTH PORTAL LIONS
**Lions Gate Bridge
Charles Marega 1939**
When unveiled, sculptor Marega's two
sphinx-like concrete lions on fluted,
moderne podiums were criticized as being too stylized, and were doubtlessly
compared with the tame courthouse
creatures (138). They do have a somewhat totalitarian demeanour, dated now,
but still disquieting. Lions Gate Bridge is
named after the 'Lions' twin peaks on
the North Shore.

237
PARK BOARD OFFICES
**Beach Avenue entrance
Underwood, McKinley & Cameron
1960**
The sensitive design of this building is
styled to fit unobtrusively into the natural setting. Projecting beams and horizontal emphasis give the building a
Japanese feel, but it is more obviously influenced by Wright and the early international style. There is an extensive use
of timber and rustic stone cladding, and
the period interior is well preserved.

238
A.C. HIRSHFIELD HOUSE
1963 Comox Street
Gamble & Kemp 1910
This craftsman style home has a characteristic shallow pitched roof, wide eaves,
projecting brackets, half-timbered gables,
and horizontal wood trim. The gables
and the absence of a porch bring a Swiss
chalet smile to the design.

239
THE PRESIDIO
2088 Barclay Street
Henriquez & Partners 1990-1
The Presidio is the Sylvia Hotel extension (243) revisited but lacking the latter's humour and raison d'être. There
was no heritage building to refer to here
so the architect imported one – an
Adolf Loos house in Europe – which, de-
constructed in a rather self-regarding
manner, informs the Presidio's design.

240
HUNTINGTON WEST
1995 Beach Avenue
Reno Negrin & Associates 1973
In this uncompromising example of the
brutalist style, precast concrete is assembled in an abstract, geometric pattern expressing the force of raw materials employed in a crude, almost vernacular, manner, curiously attuned to the
city's rugged periphery.

241
EUGENIA PLACE
1919 Beach Avenue
Henriquez & Partners 1988-90
This postmodern palazzo, with its astonishingly bold oriel and saucer-shaped roof deck (the tree refers to the height of the original forest), is alive with invention. The troglodyte entrance and watery landscaping planted with petrified tree stumps (along with deconstructivist site planning) intended to define the previous buildings on the site, pose puzzling metaphors.

242
SYLVIA HOTEL
1154 Gilford Street
W.P. White 1912
Once a landmark for ships approaching the harbour, the Sylvia looks more like a gigantic piece of topiary than a hotel. Virginia creeper, planted by one of the original residents of the then Sylvia Court Apartments, completely covers the façade. Neoclassical terracotta on the top floor and cornice, and a general old-fashioned, European ambience maintain the hotel's popularity.

243
SYLVIA HOTEL EXTENSION
1861 Beach Avenue
Henriquez & Partners 1987
This definitive example of postmodernism, layered with meaning and subtle statement, skilfully overcomes a problematic site squeezed between the Sylvia (242) and Ocean Towers (by Rix Reinecke 1958). Glazed, angled modernism emerging from an Edwardian pastiche invests the new design with a mischievous, sceptical reference to the past.

244

ALEXANDRA PARK BAND-STAND
1700-block Beach Avenue
1914

This fanciful Edwardian bandstand evokes the vanished imperial age of brass bands and civilized leisure. It has a two-tiered octagonal design with vigorous, scrolled brackets branching from stout cedar roof supports. Comfortable in its wooded setting, it is the only survivor of seven bandstands of the era which once graced city parks.

245

BEACH TOWERS
1600-block Beach Avenue
C.B.K. Van Norman & Associates
1964-5, 1968

Three towers (a fourth later added) comprise this 1960s high-rise cluster, the first of its type in Vancouver. Rising from a podium and car park, this project shows the influence of Le Corbusier's radical 1930s planning theories (now out of vogue but being reconsidered) by which cluttered old neighbourhoods were to be replaced by a utopia of highways, point towers, and plazas.

246

KENSINGTON PLACE
1386 Nicola Street
Phillip M. Julian 1912-13

This flamboyant Italianate apartment block looks like it should be on the shores of Lake Garda. There is a suggestion of fin-de-siècle Milan in the heavily bracketed cornice (which includes a pack of ferocious lion heads) and adventurous use of concrete, especially on the baroque wedding cake doorway. Columned balconies and ceremonial iron lamp standards add to the heady concoction.

247
GABRIOLA
1531 Davie Street
Samuel Maclure 1900-1

Maclure, the darling of Vancouver's and Victoria's plutocracy, designed this mansion (now a restaurant) for sugar magnate B.T. Rogers. Richly textured sandstone quarried on nearby Gabriola Island is composed and carved in eccentric friezes in eclectic Victorian style which is repeated in the sumptuous baronial interior (outstanding pre-Raphaelite style stained glass by James Bloomfield).

248
THE BEAUFORT
1160 Nicola Street
1932

Mock-Tudor's enduring appeal continues to this day, long after the decline of the British Empire. Suburban subdivisions are still styled in this cozy, picturesque fashion but are, architecturally, less assured than this individual example with its overhung central bay, leaded glass, and ersatz heraldry. Incongruous but exquisite art nouveau tiles decorate the entrance.

249
PENDRELL APARTMENTS
1419 Pendrell Street
C.P. Jones 1910

This urbane Georgian revival work would be companionable on the streets of Bristol or Boston. Graceful bow windows, precise brickwork and cornice, and an art nouveau stained glass stairway window enhance the façade. Directly east is the Thomas A. Fee house (by Parr & Fee 1904), notable for its turreted features and current state of dilapidation.

250
THE QUEEN CHARLOTTE
1101 Nicola Street
Dominion Construction 1928

This exuberant Spanish colonial revival concrete apartment block blends Raymond Chandler's southern California of the period and the European belle époque. A 2-storey moorish-tiled entrance, with original bevelled glass and Castilian light fittings, leads to an art deco detailed lobby, complete with a vintage concertina-gated elevator. Note the imitative infill at 1525 Pendrell.

251
LORD ROBERTS SCHOOL
1100 Bidwell Street
W.T. Whiteway 1907

This is a well-preserved example of Italianate design. Round-arched windows, campanile-like twin towers, and a continuous cornice are the hallmarks of the style, used in the same way at Seymour School (67), built the same year.

252
1050 Nicola Street
c. 1906

The gabled front, wide-brimmed eaves, stained glass, and bay window within a classically columned porch are typical features on this Edwardian home, a rare survivor in the West End. The period aura is enhanced in the garden. The twin holly bushes and the maturing monkey puzzle tree (a then fashionable planting imported from South America) were planted when the house was built.

253
FIRE HALL NO. 6
1500 Nelson Street
Honeyman & Curtis 1907-8
This is the first fire station in North America specifically designed for motorized equipment. The almost pagoda style, tiled roof, and strong horizontal emphasis, in contrast to the Italianate hose tower, bring an unexpected, and probably unintended, whiff of early Wright to this design, restored in 1989.

254
BARCLAY MANOR
1447 Barclay Street
1904
One of nine heritage homes, including the Roedde House (255), restored as Barclay Square Heritage Park, a 1980s city and Heritage Canada initiative planned by Downs/Archambault and carried out by the Iredale Partnership, Barclay Manor was built for Frank Baynes, manager of the Dominion Hotel in Gastown (12). A striking gable sequence with delicate gingerbread detail surmounts a curvaceous, columned verandah.

255
ROEDDE HOUSE MUSEUM
1415 Barclay Street
1892-3
A delightful Queen Anne house, this design has been cautiously attributed to Francis Rattenbury of Victoria's Empress Hotel and Parliament Buildings and Vancouver's Court House (137) fame. Most houses of this type were the work of local builders but the Jacobean turret, part of Rattenbury's vocabulary, seems to have been drawn by a professional pen.

256
ST. PAUL'S PARISH CHURCH
1138 Jervis Street
1905

The original St. Paul's Mission Church was moved on skids from Yaletown up newly cleared Davie Street by a team of horses in 1895, but it was replaced by the present wooden Gothic revival building to serve a growing congregation. Unassuming from the outside, the church contains a splendid hand-built Gothic interior, not unlike that in Christ Church Cathedral (182).

257
TUDOR MANOR
1311 Beach Avenue
Townley & Matheson 1927-8,
Paul Merrick 1987-8

Tudor Manor is the result of misguided heritage preservation, not so much because the original façade's pleasing street frontage has been retained but more because its style, bogus in 1928, has been used to ornament the otherwise elegant 1988 tower which shoots up behind in twenty storeys of crenellated pseudo-medievalism.

258
PACIFIC HEIGHTS HOUSING CO-OPERATIVE
1035 Pacific Street
Roger Hughes 1983-5

These buildings integrate old and new where Tudor Manor (257) so conspicuously fails. Modern infill acts as a theatrical backdrop for a row of rehabilitated Edwardian homes without sacrificing its own identity. The eye-catching elevator tower, layered passages, and semi-private enclosures create a village perché ambience in keeping with the area's steep topography.

Bric-à-brac from an industrial past has been retained.

Granville Island

Area Seven **FALSE CREEK SOUTH**

ORDERING the downtown peninsula on the south lies False Creek, a tidal inlet that once covered a thousand acres, nearly four times its present size. It extended as far east as Clark Drive and, at high tide, joined Burrard Inlet at Columbia Street. At the site of present-day Main Street, a short boat ride connected the young Gastown to the Westminster Trail (now Kingsway).

In 1872 a bridge was built at the narrows and development began 'across the creek.' Loggers were the first to move in and by 1874 had clearcut much of the Fairview area. Homes, stores, and factories soon followed. Settlement of Mount Pleasant (the area between Clark Drive and Cambie and north of 16th Avenue) began in the 1880s, and Fairview (north of 16th from Cambie to about Burrard) was officially named and opened for settlement in 1890.

The CPR originally intended to develop its yards along the south shore of False Creek. But Vancouver's merchants, fearing that a rival town might be established, convinced city hall to offer the railway a 20-year exemption from taxes in return for locating on the north shore of

left: *A spine of clerestory windows illuminate a vigorous timber interior in this West 1st Avenue industrial relic.*

right: *The old Canadian National Railway Station, built on landfill at the head of False Creek*

the creek. It appeared that industry would be confined to the north side of False Creek while the south shore would remain residential.

However, in 1902 the CPR laid a branch line along the south shore, opening the way for industrial development. In 1903 BC Mills, Timber & Trading Company shifted its main plant to the area, and was followed by others who were drawn by the area's ample supplies of fresh water, its rail access, and its convenient harbour. At the eastern end of False Creek, the Great Northern and the Canadian Northern Railways acquired terminal rights, and the entire eastern third of the waterway was filled to provide land for yards and stations. The federal government entered the scene in 1915 with the creation of Granville Island. By then, False Creek had shrunk to about one-quarter of its original size and what remained was occupied by log booms and lined with smoke-belching mills and factories.

In the late 1960s the city finally decided that something had to be done with this decaying industrial eyesore in the heart of the city. Many industrial plants had relocated and a rash of fires plagued the rundown

creosote- and grease-coated plants that remained. In 1971 the False Creek Study Group, composed of private consultants and city officials, began to investigate redevelopment possibilities for the land around the creek, most of which was owned by the three levels of government and the CPR. Early discussions resulted in a massive land swap, with the CPR withdrawing to the north shore of the creek, leaving the province in control of its eighty-five acres along the south shore. The province then deeded the land to the city in return for a city-owned parcel on Burnaby Mountain (the site of Simon Fraser University). Thompson, Berwick, Pratt & Partners were selected in 1974 to prepare a preliminary scheme, and construction on the city-owned land soon began.

At the western end of the creek, the federal government began the redevelopment of Granville Island by transferring the island from the National Harbours Board to the Canada Mortgage & Housing Corporation (CMHC). An advisory board, the Granville Island Trust, was established to oversee the project, and Norman Hotson was appointed architect.

259
SEAFORTH ARMORY
1650 Burrard Street
McCarter & Nairne 1935
This landmark Scots Baronial castle (in poured concrete) makes a fanciful yet appropriate home for the Seaforth Highlanders of Canada. Two round towers guard the entrance; castellations and corner turrets suggest defensive strength; and cast thistles on the finials allude to the regiment's spiritual home. The coat-of-arms above the entry is by sculptor Charles Marega.

260
MARKTREND BUILDING
1650 West 2nd Avenue
Busby Bridger 1991
This crisp, high-tech office building, built around a central courtyard, recalls early modernist ideas in its exposed steel beams and use of industrial materials. It is designed for the addition of apartment units on the third floor when impending zoning changes permit. The louvred corner sections conceal the building's mechanical services.

261
GRANVILLE ISLAND PUBLIC MARKET
1689 Johnston Street
Rehabilitated by Norman Hotson
1979-80
The bustling public market is the heart of Granville Island's redevelopment and best illustrates the overall design approach. The tin sheds that once housed Wright's Ropes and BC Equipment were saved and recycled. Large doors and areas of glazing were emphasized, and even the overhead, travelling cranes were left in place as a reminder of the building's industrial past.

262

CREEKHOUSE
1551 Johnston Street
Rehabilitated by Brian Johnston
(designer) 1971-2

While politicians were still debating the island's future, developers Mitch Taylor and Bill Harvey began rehabilitation of an abandoned Monsanto Chemical warehouse. Their decision to use the same corrugated tin cladding set the tone for future conversions. Taylor and Harvey were also the founders of the Granville Island Brewery, the first new industry on the island in decades.

263

OCEAN CEMENT
1415 Johnston Street
c. 1919-20

Ocean Cement (originally Diether's Coal and Building Supplies) is the last large-scale industry left on this man-made industrial island, created during the First World War. The blend of industrial, commercial, and cultural activities (and of pedestrian and vehicular traffic) was once much criticized, but it is a large part of the island's dynamism and vitality.

264

EMILY CARR COLLEGE OF ART AND DESIGN
1399 Johnston Street
Rehabilitated by Howard/Yano
1979-80

Attracting cultural and institutional tenants, like the former Vancouver School of Art, was deemed an essential part of Granville Island's success. Architect Ron Howard linked the former Westex Industries and British Ropes buildings with new construction that uses the industrial corrugated tin siding, skylights, and exposed beams characteristic of other structures on the island.

265
GRANVILLE ISLAND BREWERY
1441 Cartwright Street
Rehabilitated by Boak Alexander
1984

A modest moderne industrial building, but a paradise for beer drinkers where buying a six-pack has the added attraction of being able to see the workings of the brewery inside. This is a good example of one of the guiding principles of the island's development: bringing people in on the action. Public tours are held at 1:00 and 3:00 PM daily.

266
FALSE CREEK HOUSING CO-OPERATIVE
918-1072 Scantlings Street, 951-99 Lamey's Mill Road
Henriquez & Todd 1975-7

Near the Laurel Street Crossing, a landscaped pedestrian bridge 1976-7) that links the False Creek development with the Fairview Slopes, and separated by Charleson Park, are two groups of red-roofed townhouses developed by the False Creek Co-operative Housing Association. An award-winning elementary school (also by Henriquez & Todd 1977-8) is integrated into the complex.

267
807-44 Sawcut Street, 800-40 Millbank Street
Thompson, Berwick, Pratt & Partners 1975-7

This cluster of townhouses perhaps best expresses the vision of False Creek as expressed by the architects in their original plan. A village-like intimacy is achieved by breaking up the composition with advancing and retreating walls, varying roof heights, and the interplay of rooflets, chimneys, and fences.

268
682-98 Millbank Street
Rhone & Iredale 1975-7
These aluminum and glass condominiums, with their long planar façade, uniform roofline, and high-tech detailing,
depart from the overall design concept
as originally evisaged by the co-ordinat-
ing architects, Thompson, Berwick &
Pratt, but they have an urbanity and
stylish seaside feeling that some of the
other developments lack.

269
LEG-IN-BOOT SQUARE
Thompson, Berwick & Pratt 1974
Named for the dismembered leg that
was once washed up on the shore near
here, Leg-in-Boot Square was designed
as the central shopping area for the new
False Creek development. Other street
names – Greenchain, Sawcut, Millyard,
Scantlings, Foundry – recall images of
False Creek's former industrial character, especially the shipbuilding and
sawmills.

270
OPSAL STEEL
97 East 2nd Avenue
T.H. Bamforth 1918
Built for Columbia Block and Tool by
Dominion Construction, this heavy-timber framed factory is typical of early
False Creek industrial buildings, and one
of the few to survive. The moderne 2-
storey corner office building is a later
addition and features some distinctive
1940s graphics, particularly the company's name in steel lettering above the
door.

271
SCIENCE WORLD
1455 Quebec Street
1984-6
The 'golf ball' is a 15-storey geodesic sphere of stainless steel surrounded by an outer frame of white steel beams. A legacy of Expo '86, it served as the Expo Preview Centre, and after extensive re-fitting and additions in 1988-9 (by Boak Alexander), it became Science World. An Omnimax Theatre fills the central dome.

272
VIA RAIL STATION
1150 Station Street
Pratt & Ross 1917-19
The Canadian Northern Railway, the second transcontinental railroad, obtained terminal rights on False Creek in return for extensive concessions to the city, including the construction of a large downtown hotel (Hotel Vancouver, 181). It is currently undergoing renovation and will soon become a combined bus and train terminal.

273
CANADA PACKERS BUILDING
750 Terminal Avenue
Eric R. Arthur 1937
The only Vancouver building by Eric Arthur who, as professor of design at the University of Toronto School of Architecture, introduced Ned Pratt, Bob Berwick, and a number of other young architects to the international style. Here, international style meets moderne in a striking and influential industrial building for Canada Packers.

274
NATIVE EDUCATION CENTRE
285 East 5th Avenue
Larry McFarland 1985

Inspired by the traditional Haida long-house, huge wood posts support what are probably the largest solid wood beams in Vancouver building history – 13.2 metres long and 30 x 80 centimetres in cross-section – which were custom-cut from old growth Douglas fir trees. The ceremonial entrance totem pole is by master carver Norman Tait of the Nishga. The centre is run by the Urban Native Indian Educational Society.

275
BREWERY CREEK BUILDING
280 East 6th Avenue
1903-4

Charles Doering, owner of the Stag and Pheasant Hotel on Water Street, and partner Otto Marstrand opened this brick and stone industrial building in 1904 as part of their expanding brewery operation. It featured electric bottle-washing machinery and an artificial-ice making plant. Other brewers, in search of clean fresh water soon followed Doering's lead, hence the name, Brewery Creek.

276
WESTERN FRONT LODGE
303 East 8th Avenue
1922

The Western Front, an artists' collective specializing in video and media art, acquired this former Knights of Pythias Lodge in 1973 and converted it to gallery and performance space, production facilities, and some living quarters. The metal installation on the side wall, by Alan Storey (1983) and called 'Machine for Bad Weather,' spins engagingly when it rains.

277
LEDINGHAM HOUSE
2425 Brunswick Street
1895
One of the oldest surviving houses in Mount Pleasant, this Queen Anne home is now the centrepiece of Ledingham Place (by Edward de Grey 1988), a housing project developed by the First United Church. The property originally contained two other listed houses: one was demolished to make way for the complex; the other, which the developers had planned to retain, burned down during construction.

278
QUEBEC MANOR
101 East 7th Avenue
Townsend & Townsend 1912
Two immodest female figures energetically support the heavy pediment that forms the frontispiece of this marvellous 4-storey apartment building. Originally the Mt. Stephen Apartments, it features diamond-patterned red and yellow brickwork, a heavy, bracketed cornice, wrought-iron balconies, and a tiled entrance hall with an elaborate, double-height, wooden baroque screen acting as an inner door.

279
LEE BUILDING
175 East Broadway
Stroud and Keith 1912
For many years the largest commercial building outside the downtown core, the Lee Building, like Heritage Hall (282) and the Walden Building (409), is a symbol of the high aspirations once held (but never realized) for the Mount Pleasant area. A block north, at 2403 Main Street, is a Woolworth's store that has retained its original maroon and gold sign.

280
CHRISTIAN CITY CHURCH
85 East 10th Avenue
Parr & Fee 1909-10
Originally the Mount Pleasant Presbyterian Church, this building combines Romanesque revival entrance arches and corner turret with late Gothic depressed, pointed arches. This eclectic mix is brought together by brickwork trimmed with stone. The 1894 meeting hall (now covered in brick-pattern synthetic siding) still stands at the western end of the church property.

281
MOUNT PLEASANT BAPTIST CHURCH
2600 Quebec Street
Burke, Horwood & White 1909-10
In contrast to the ponderous solidity of the Christian City Church across the road, this handsome Tudor revival church has a light, informal feel. In 1912 the building was raised on jacks, given a quarter turn, and set on a new foundation; a stone tower, quite similar to that of the First Baptist Church (211), was also added.

282
HERITAGE HALL
3102 Main Street
Archibald Campbell Hope 1914-16
For many years this pleasantly eclectic Edwardian confection, with its rusticated stone base, coupled pilasters, steep roof, and tall corner clock tower, sat like a beached ocean liner in empty, isolated splendour. Originally built as Postal Station C, and occupied for a time by the RCMP, it is now a community arts and social centre.

283
'ISIS' AND 'ISIS COTTAGE'
122-26 West 10th Avenue
1907

In 1987 builder Richard Fearn repro-
duced the original 'cast stone' blocks of
this unusual Edwardian era house to re-
construct the front porch and to build
Isis Cottage, the attractive infill dwelling
at the rear. Much of the detailing of the
original house, such as the rusticated
quoins and arched inset balcony, are mirrored in the cottage. The project received a City of Vancouver Heritage
Award in 1991.

284
DAVIS HOUSE
166 West 10th Avenue
1891

This lovely streetscape of Queen Anne
and Edwardian houses benefited from the
efforts of the Davis family who, in the
mid-1970s, restored this simple home
with its bay window, 2-storey porch, and
carpenter's detailing. They went on to
restore virtually all the homes on the
south side of the block. In recognition
they received a City of Vancouver Heritage Award in 1980 and a Heritage Canada Award the following year.

285
LABOUR TEMPLE
307 West Broadway
1949

The bas-relief sculpture above the entrance – an heroic art deco vision of the
nobility of labour – was created by BC
sculptor Beatrice Lennie, a student of
Charles Marega (see 236, 288, 307), and
one of the first women graduates of the
Vancouver School of Art. The letters in
the lower corners refer to the Trade
Labour Congress and the American
Federation of Labor.

286
McLEAN HOUSE
356 West 11th Avenue
Campbell & Bennett 1910

This grand Queen Anne home of brick and stone features granite quoins and sills, a generous porch with fine carpenter's detailing, and a corner turret. As in Fairview or Grandview, the development of this section of Mount Pleasant as an élite residential area effectively came to an end with the opening of Shaughnessy Heights.

287
410 West 12th Avenue
Parr & Fee 1909

Winner of a Vancouver Heritage Award for restoration, this Parr & Fee house features a domed tower (nearly identical to the twin towers of 'Glen Brae' (330), built the following year), a rich variety of surface treatment, and roof brackets that look like a high-kicking line of Rockettes. Restoration was made viable by a heritage bonus which allowed the development of sympathetic infill.

288
CITY HALL
453 West 12th Avenue
Townley & Matheson 1935-6

After a decade of bickering, the present city hall site was chosen in 1935 with the prodding of Mayor G.G. McGeer, who wanted to strengthen links with newly annexed South Vancouver. A touch totalitarian, as was much civic architecture of the time, it is still one of the city's most engaging public buildings. The 4-storey annex is by Townley, Matheson & Partners (1968-70); the statue of George Vancouver, by Charles Marega.

289
CITY SQUARE
555 West 12th Avenue
Paul Merrick 1989

Two fine Edwardian schools, the Provincial Normal School (by Pearce & Hope 1908-9) and the Model School (by E.E. Blackmore 1905) have virtually disappeared within this new complex of shops and offices. For an example of what the enigmatic Merrick is capable of, see his small, wonderfully sensitive homage to Frank Lloyd Wright, the UBC Medical Alumni Centre (1990), a block west at 2750 Heather.

290
PROTECTION OF THE VIRGIN MARY UKRAINIAN CATHOLIC CHURCH
560 West 14th Avenue
Julian Jastremsky 1982

An exotic gilded trio of onion domes rises above this rather bland residential corner. Itinerant, New York-based architect Julian Jastremsky specializes in Ukrainian Catholic churches, interpreting the traditional domed form in a modern idiom for parishes all over North America. The stained glass is from a factory in Yonkers, New York.

291
HEATHER PAVILION
2733 Heather Street
Grant & Henderson 1903-6;
various additions 1910-59

The motley conglomeration, known today as the Heather Pavilion, started out as the Fairview Building, a distinguished granite structure with four square cupolaed towers. More than fifty years of additions – mandated by Vancover General Hospital's increasingly desperate need for accommodation – have produced this sprawling hodgepodge, in styles ranging from Georgian to Bauhaus.

292
HEALTH CENTRE FOR CHILDREN
715 West 12th Avenue
Townley & Matheson 1943-4

This is a fine example of the moderne style in public architecture. The stream-lined, cast concrete railings thrusting from a deeply recessed entry are its outstanding feature. Columnar shafts behind the entrance porch and incised shadow bands between the windows also typify the style. Other Townley & Matheson buildings at VGH in the moderne style include the Nurses' Residence (1949) and Physical Medicine (c. 1945).

293
CENTENNIAL PAVILION
855 West 12th Avenue
Townley, Matheson & Partners 1956-8

Vancouver General Hospital was incorporated in 1902 and purchased 5 1/2 acres here in Fairview to replace the small City Hospital at Beatty and Pender streets (1886). Centennial Pavilion – the largest building in the hospital complex until the completion of the BC Health Sciences Centre next door (by Hemingway Nelson 1990-2) – has a slightly old-fashioned feel, more closely related to buildings of a decade before.

294
FAIRMONT MEDICAL BUILDING
750 West Broadway
McCarter, Nairne & Partners 1960

The three towers on this busy Fairview corner, the modernist slab of the Fairmont Building, Paul Merrick's decorative postmodern office block at 777 West Broadway (1987), and the striking sculptural shape of 805 West Broadway (Vladimir Plavsic & Associates 1972-3) are a graphic illustration of the changing design approach to the composition of a tall building over the last three decades.

295
HEATHER COURT TOWNHOUSES
730 West 7th Avenue
James K.M. Cheng 1980

This award-winning townhouse development is one of a group of three on West 7th, each featuring a central court, faced with identical brick but with slight differences in detail. Architect Cheng won the Governor General's Award for the group at 704 West 7th, but the rhythmic curved balconies of 730 make it, perhaps, the most pleasing of the three.

296
975 West 8th Avenue
1905

This small survivor shares the block with several office buildings, the BC Automobile Association parking lot, a few other small houses, and a postmodern apartment block in lavender and blue stucco. Fairview has undergone a series of changes – from upper middle-class residential to working class to small-scale commercial and back to residential – all of which have left their mark on this now typical mixed-use block.

297
CONSTRUCTION HOUSE
2675 Oak Street
Gardiner & Mercer 1928

Originally the first Jewish Community Centre, it was designed to be built in two phases. The first part was completed in 1928 but, with the onset of the depression, the extension, which was to have included a gymnasium and 600-seat theatre, was never built. By the time the means were available, the centre of Jewish population had shifted south and a new centre built at 41st and Oak.

298
SIXTH ESTATE
1000-block West 6th Avenue
Roger Hughes 1982

Architect Hughes won the Governor
General's Award for this innovative project which features a quiet interior
'street' parallel to noisy West 6th
Avenue. Most of an existing complex of
warehouses was retained and the interior was opened out by demolishing two
sections, making room for inner landscaped courtyards. A sound screen of
glass blocks allows light but not noise
into the serene, contained space of the
interior.

299
TAKEHARA TENEMENTS
1017 West 7th Avenue
G. Matsuda 1913

Builder G. Yoda erected this tenement
for Japanese labourers employed in the
many sawmills along False Creek. Only
18 feet wide, the building stretches 110
feet to the rear of the property; its floor
space rivals that of a West End high rise.
It is best seen from the rear lane, where
new townhouse neighbours have picked
up the tenement's red/brown clapboard
siding.

300
HODSON MANOR
1254 West 7th Avenue
1894

In June 1974, Fairview residents were
treated to the spectacle of this fine
house being moved from its former location at 8th and Hemlock. The left and
central bays were built in 1894 for
Captain J.J. Logan, and the right side was
added in 1904 (by J.J. Honeyman) for the
11-child family of sometime alderman
and yachtsman William Hodson.

301
JAMES ENGLAND HOUSE
2300 Birch Street
1910

Fairview, on the hillside above False Creek between Granville and Cambie streets, developed rapidly after the opening of a tramline in 1891. Many fine homes, like this Queen Anne house were built in this period, but Fairview never succeeded as a high-class development because of competition from Shaughnessy Heights and the presence of a sewer outfall at the bottom of the hill.

302
CHALMERS UNITED CHURCH
2801 Hemlock Street
S.B. Bird 1911-12

This Palladian revival church is unusual in Vancouver, where 'spiritual' Gothic-derived forms were much preferred over the 'rational' classical revivals for religious buildings. Architect Samuel Buttrey Bird, who later entered into partnership with noted church architects Twizell & Twizell, won an open competition with this brick and cast concrete design which features a dome and cupola at the crossing.

303
BOBOLI
2776 Granvile Street
David Vance Design 1987

A neoclassical arched stone doorway centred in a stark glass façade makes a theatrical entrance to this upscale clothing shop. Retail design, ephemeral in nature and having more in common with set design than with architecture, achieves an illusory permanence here. The doorway itself is an upper-floor window moulding salvaged from a Mexico City office building damaged in the 1985 earthquake.

304
STANLEY THEATRE
2750 Granville Street
H.H. Simmonds 1930
The fate of this Moorish style art deco picture palace has become one of the more contentious of recent heritage issues in Vancouver. Although proposed development calls for the restoration of the façade to its 1930s appearance, a restrictive covenant prevents any future buyer from showing films here. At issue is the building's meaning to the community and its cultural role.

305
TERMINAL CITY LAWN BOWLING CLUB
3025 Fir Street
1920
The arcaded pavilion of the Terminal City Lawn Bowling Club looks like something out of British India, a polo club perhaps. The name reflects the city's pride in being the western terminus of the transcontinental railway and an important stop on the CPR's 'All Red Route,' that circled the globe linking the far-flung holdings of the British Empire.

306
MADRONA APARTMENTS
1575 West 15th Avenue
c. 1925
South Granville is an established neighbourhood of 3-floor walk-up apartments (with some high-rise intrusions), all much the same in plan but dressed up in varying stylistic finery – the Madrona, for example, in Spanish revival. Across the street the Mount Royal (by Gardiner & Mercer 1927) wears a Tudor look. Unity of scale and variety of design give the area a comfortable urbanity.

Voluptuous domed towers

and a theatrical

Corinthian-columned porch

Glen Brae

Area Eight   **SHAUGHNESSY**

THE Canadian Pacific Railway announced in 1907 that a 250-acre portion of its immense land holdings south of False Creek would be cleared and developed as an exclusive residential area. The subdivision was to be called Shaughnessy Heights after CPR president Sir Thomas Shaughnessy. The timing was perfect. With the opening (in 1909) of a new Granville Street Bridge and the proliferation of apartment buildings and commercial development in the previously exclusive West End, the city's moneyed classes were eager to move to the new development.

Shaughnessy Heights was laid out by Danish engineer L.E. Davick and Montreal landscape architect Frederick Todd with tree-lined streets and boulevards that curve along the natural contours of the land following the fashion set by American landscape architect Frederick Law Olmsted (the designer of Central Park in New York and Mount Royal Park in Montreal) and the garden city movement in England. Many of the streets – Angus, Marpole, Osler, Hosmer, and Nanton, among others – were named after CPR officials. The area was

subdivided into lots that varied in size from one-fifth of an acre to one-and-one-half acres. The railway set a minimum price of $6,000 for any house built and offered generous loans to encourage construction.

The first lots were sold in 1909. After two more years of stump clearing and another of road building, fine homes began to appear throughout the area. The most popular style was the Tudor revival, with its connotations of English gentry, though other styles were exploited as well. Within two decades, virtually every influential family in Vancouver had moved to Shaughnessy Heights. In 1922 the provincial government passed the Shaughnessy Heights Building Restriction Act, limiting the area to single-family homes and discouraging the further subdivision of properties. Shaughnessy was extended south to 33rd and then to 41st Avenue, but the newer areas never achieved the exclusivity of the original section.

The depression of the 1930s hit the area hard. Many residents could no longer afford to maintain expensive homes and the area came to be known, perhaps with a certain satisfaction, as 'Poverty Hill' or

Shaughnessy is a potpourri of residential styles ranging from Spanish colonial revival haciendas (left, The Crescent and Angus Drive) to Georgian revival/federal style homes (right, Marguerite Street).

'Mortgage Heights.' At the beginning of the Second World War, houses stood empty and deteriorating in a time of severe housing shortage. Emergency wartime legislation was passed to permit the conversion of such residences into rooming houses. Indeed, Hycroft became a veterans' hospital. All shared homes operating in 1955 were permitted by law to remain that way, but new rental suites were banned.

In the 1970s the city recognized the onerous burden that strict single-family zoning placed on some Shaughnessy property owners. It was becoming increasingly difficult to maintain such large properties as single-family homes, but legislation prevented their conversion to apartments or other economically viable uses. In 1981 innovative new zoning and development by-laws and design guidelines were introduced which attempted to recognize these economic realities while maintaining the area's unique historical, architectural, and landscape qualities. To this end, limited subdivision, well-designed and appropriate infill housing, and suitable institutional conversions are actively encouraged.

307
HYCROFT
1489 McRae Avenue
Thomas Hooper 1909-12

The most imposing mansion in Shaughnessy, Hycroft was built for General Alexander Duncan McRae, a future senator with interests in lumbering, fishing, coal, and real estate. Six majestic columns, repeated to the north overlooking an Italian garden, support a grand porte-cochère. The interior plasterwork is by sculptor Charles Marega. Since 1962 it has been the home of the University Women's Club.

308
WALTER C. NICHOL HOUSE
1402 The Crescent
Maclure and Fox 1912-13

Tudor revival was the favoured style in Shaughnessy Heights, evoking visions of the English country manor and its attendant culture, gentility, and wealth. The voluminous roofs with broad eaves and tall chimneys of this superb house for *Province* publisher (and later Lieutenant Governor) Nichol are typical of houses by the renowned Victoria architect Samuel Maclure and his Vancouver partner C.C. Fox.

309
HENRY M. LEGGAT HOUSE
1363 The Crescent
c. 1911

This attractive house recalls an 18th-century New England Georgian townhouse with its pedimented three-part façade, pilastered clapboard walls, hipped roof, curved entrance porch, and shuttered sash windows; although the flat façade characteristic of houses south of the border is here broken by projecting bows with windows of fine curved glass.

310
FREDERICK M. KELLY HOUSE
1398 The Crescent
Townley & Matheson 1921

A Dutch colonial revival fashion swept Vancouver in the 1920s and this Townley & Matheson design, built on grade, is an early example of the trend. The second-floor windows appear as an extended dormer in the double-sloped mansard roof. Here stucco has graduated from half-timber infill status to a full-fledged facing material in its own right.

311
GEORGE E. MacDONALD HOUSE ('THE HOLLIES')
1350 The Crescent
1914

A columned, pedimented portico intro-duces a classical revival house that would not be out of place in the eastern U.S. Yet the mixture of sources – Greek Ionic capitals, Roman semicircular pediments, and a 'Palladian' window in the pediment – and the silhouette-breaking dormer windows show an indifference to ac-cepted rules of composition in a way that is typical of Canadian architecture.

312
BRYCE W. FLECK HOUSE
1296 The Crescent
Honeyman & Curtis 1929

This house, for industrial supplier Fleck, and the nearby C. Carry House at 1232 The Crescent (also probably by Honey-man & Curtis 1929) show the persis-tence of the Tudor revival style. Stucco has taken over from wood as the princi-pal surface material. The porte-cochère, bay windows, stained glass, and curved gable above the entrance are attractive features.

313
M.Y. AIVAZOFF HOUSE ('VILLA RUSSE')
3390 The Crescent
Cleven Cox 1921

Russian emigré financier and patron of the arts Misak Y. Aivazoff built this retreat and entertained lavishly (visiting Russian nobility and artists, including Grand Duke Alexander and Serge Rachmaninoff were guests) until he lost everything in the depression. A later resident of this elegant classical villa was BC Electric Company chairman Dal Grauer who added the front terrace.

314
L.W. SHATFORD HOUSE
3338 The Crescent
1912

Broker and former MLA Lytton W. Shatford built this particularly fine example of the craftsman style. Love for wood is evident in the shingled siding and the generous ornament. Projecting rafters, heavy brackets beneath the eaves, second-storey overhang and sills, and the entrance piers all exploit the decorative use of timber and emphasis on carpenter's detail, characteristic of the style.

315
FRANK L. BUCKLEY HOUSE ('IOWA')
3498 Osler Street
MacKenzie & Ker 1913

An effective and original compromise between craftsman and classical influences is reached in this fine house for lumberman Buckley. The simple three-bay façade with a central gable derives from the American Gothic cottages of A.J. Downing. The porch and entablature, however, reflect Roman ornament. Leaded glass windows and fine decorative woodwork show a high level of craftsmanship.

316

HUMPHREY SIMMONS HOUSE ('GREY GABLES')
1251 Matthews Avenue
possibly M.H. Baillie Scott 1910

The architect of this handsome house, with its asymmetrical gable and rough-cast stucco, and its striking coach-house gate, is unknown, but there is some evidence to suggest that it was designed by M. H. Baillie Scott, a master of the English arts and crafts style who was strongly influenced by C.F.A. Voysey and the art nouveau movement.

317

A.E. TULK HOUSE ('ROSEMARY')
3689 Selkirk Street
Maclure & Fox 1913-15

This magnificent house was named 'Rosemary' after lawyer and liquor magnate Tulk's only daughter. The half-timbering in which Samuel Maclure excelled is combined with white shingles, brown clapboard, and brick to give the appearance of having been built over generations like a rambling English manor. During the lengthy construction, the Tulks inhabited the small wing at the north end (by D.R. Paterson 1912).

318

WILLIAM ASTLELY HOUSE
3638 Osler Street
1912

This rustic and secluded bungalow with its cross-gable, generous full-width porch, and river-stone foundation and piers has an informality and sense of comfort derived from the ideals of the English arts and crafts movement and the craftsman style of Gustav Stickley or Greene and Greene. The 'California bungalow' is a more modest version of the style.

319
MONSTER HOUSES
1000-block West 27th Avenue
1988-9

This group of three is typical of the kind of large house built to maximize floor space and site coverage and which is characterized by a pastiche of 'period' detailing (often featuring an overblown double-height entry). The 'monster house' has been sharply criticized for its intrusion into the fabric of existing neighbourhoods. The banality of its design is probably its worst feature.

320
VANDUSEN BOTANICAL GARDEN PAVILION
Oak Street and 37th Avenue
Underwood, McKinley, Wilson & Smith 1975

The provincial and municipal governments and the Vancouver Foundation sponsored this 55-acre garden (formerly a golf course), named after philanthropist Whitford J. VanDusen. The Board of Parks and Recreation directed landscape development. Entry is through the pavilion, an elegant exposition of the West Coast post-and-beam style that blends seamlessly into the landscape.

321
SHAUGHNESSY PLACE
4900 Cartier Street
McCarter, Nairne & Partners 1976

Beautifully sited on the crest of a hill overlooking the VanDusen Garden – and best seen from the garden or from the lane south of 33rd Avenue – Shaughnessy Place was developed by CP's Marathon Realty. The V-shaped building has 71 suites on 6 levels. Its concrete walls (now somewhat stained) and casual building-block arrangement are reminiscent of Moshe Safdie's Habitat in Montreal.

322
ST. JOHN'S (SHAUGHNESSY) ANGLICAN CHURCH
1490 Nanton Avenue
G.L. Thornton Sharp 1949

Much of the fine detailing of this Gothic-inspired moderne church lays hidden under a layer of asphalt siding installed shortly after the church was built to combat leakage. Roman brick above the bullet windows (and in bands on the tower and body of the church) and red tile sills were uncovered during the current round of restoration begun in 1990.

323
WILLIAM WALSH HOUSE
3589 Granville Street
H. Murray 1912

Fine iron cresting caps the ridge of this stone and shingle home. (Many Vancouver buildings lost their decorative ironwork during wartime scrap metal drives.) A broad, hipped roof with flared eaves and strong horizontal emphasis – perhaps influenced by Samuel Maclure – rests on brackets. The walls are picturesquely broken by various projections and a corner turret reminiscent of the Queen Anne style.

324
ARTHUR BRENCHLEY HOUSE
3351 Granville Street
Maclure & Fox 1912

This home for wholesale grocer Arthur Brenchley is the best Vancouver representative of the kind of middle-sized Tudor revival house for which Samuel Maclure became famous in Victoria. Here, half-timbering is reduced to vertical strips of dark wood alternating with stucco rectangles on the upper floor and beneath the central gable.

325
JOHN WEST HOUSE
3290-6 Granville Street
1911

The first house to be converted to condominiums under the First Shaughnessy Development Plan, this mission style mansion (now called The Five Cedars) features a red tile roof, prominent shaped gables, and a ground-floor colonnade, all common features of the style. Compare this with the fine Spanish colonial revival house (c. 1914), a half-block south at 1499 Angus Drive.

326
ANGUS PLACE
1660 Angus Drive
3610-30 Alexandra Street
Tanner/Kay 1973

The design of this 'four-house village' consciously combines modern and traditional elements. Stark white walls and shed roofs sport such features as panelled doors with fanlights and whimsical arches – a preview of the kind of playfulness and ironic juxtaposition of elements that has come to be called postmodern. The four units face away from the street towards a communal pool and sauna.

327
W.F. SALSBURY HOUSE
1790 Angus Drive
A.A. Cox 1912

The white roughcast walls, prominent shaped gables, and deep balcony link this unusual house to the mission style. The picturesque massing and broad roofs, however, betray the influence of old English buildings on the architect. William F. Salsbury, who arrived in BC on the first transcontinental train, was one of the many CPR officials who settled in Shaughnessy Heights.

328
W.F HUNTTING HOUSE
3689 Angus Drive
Maclure & Fox 1911

The horizontally proportioned rough-cast façade, terminated at each end by a cross-gable and topped by a steep roof, resembles houses by English arts and crafts architect F.A. Voysey, teacher of Cecil Croker Fox. Here Fox is seen emerging from the Tudor shadow of his senior partner, Samuel Maclure. Two recent infill houses (by Raymond Ching 1985-6) in the once extensive grounds mirror the massing and details of the main house.

329
R.S. LENNIE HOUSE
1737 Matthews Avenue
Sharp & Thompson 1912

G.L.T. Sharp and C.J. Thompson, the original partners of a firm that has dominated Vancouver architecture for almost eighty years (known today as Hemingway Nelson), began their fertile careers as traditional revivalists. Their Georgian revival Vancouver Club (167), Gothic revival church (St. Mary's, Kerrisdale, 369), and this large Tudor revival house display the range of their styles.

330
WILLIAM LAMONT TAIT HOUSE ('GLEN BRAE')
1690 Matthews Avenue
Parr & Fee 1910

Two voluptuous domed towers and a theatrical Corinthian-columned porch make this one of the most unforgettable of Shaughnessy homes. The superb cast-iron fence was manufactured in Scotland by Walter McFarlane of Glasgow. 'Glen Brae' was bequeathed to the city in 1991 – a gift which helped establish the city's heritage foundation.

331
JOHN HENDRY HOUSE
3802 Angus Drive
Maclure & Fox 1912-15

Lumber magnate John Hendry, a native of New Brunswick who came to BC in 1873 to work at the Moodyville Sawmill and became president of BC Mills, left his large West End mansion for this enormous Tudor revival house in the new subdivision of Shaughnessy. The former coach house at the south end of the original lot, also in the Tudor revival style, has been converted into a private home.

332
B.T. LEA HOUSE
4051 Marguerite Street
John A. Pauw 1930

The continuous horizontal lines and broad overhanging roofs of this angled corner house reveal the influence of Frank Lloyd Wright. Other prairie style features are the many doors linking inside with out, and the elimination of the basement. Transient Dutch architect Pauw offers a pleasing contrast of materials with the variegated brick ground floor, wood upper storey, and shingle roof.

333
RONALD McDONALD HOUSE
4116 Angus Drive
1936

Owned and operated by the Ronald McDonald House Society as a residence for the parents of children undergoing treatment at nearby Children's Hospital, the house now features 15 bedrooms and 11 bathrooms. Architect Gary Davis (1983) added a large skylight and opened up one side of the house with a 2-storey glass conservatory to provide a light and airy feel.

334
A.B. WEEKS HOUSE
1808 West King Edward Avenue
1923

The mission style, which developed in the American Southwest, gained popularity in Vancouver in the 1920s. This modest (by Shaughnessy standards) white stucco residence recalls the long, low profile, tiled roofs, and repetitive shaped gables of its California model. The south side of King Edward Avenue marks the beginning of the second Shaughnessy subdivision.

335
HALTERMAN HOUSE
5391 Angus Drive
C.B.K. Van Norman 1937

Charles Van Norman, an Ontarian trained at the University of Manitoba, designed several 'Cape Cod cottages,' including this charming brick-and-wood example. The simple forms (albeit in period style) prepared the way for the 1940s modernism of such architects as Bob Berwick, Ned Pratt, Peter Thornton, and Van Norman himself.

336
J. BROOKS HOUSE
5055 Connaught Drive
1920

By 1920, Shaughnessy Heights was almost completely filled and work was begun on the second and third Shaughnessy subdivisions. Though homes here were generally more modest, some like this Cotswald cottage grown giant, rival anything in the original development. The high side gable roof, with an undulating shingle covering that mimics the thatch of its English model, is its outstanding feature.

337
J.A. COLLINS HOUSE
5326 Connaught Drive
Townley & Matheson 1929

This elegantly proportioned and finely detailed Georgian revival house was built for Fraser Valley Tie and Timber Company manager, J.A. Collins. The basement was fitted out as a rustic log cabin for the Collins's square dance evenings with an alcove for the caller and a horsehair-sprung dance floor. Matheson's own house, a dignified exercise in Norman revival (1929), is a half-block north at 5237 Connaught.

338
ERIC HAMBER HOUSE
('GREENCROFT')
3838 Cypress Street
1912-13

Built for banker (later lieutenant governor) Eric Hamber and his bride, the daughter of John Hendry, this beautiful and unusual house features a large château-style tower, wooden colonnade, and a conservatory. Among his many achievements, Hamber captained the Toronto Argonaut football, hockey, and rowing teams. He was also chancellor of UBC from 1944 until 1951.

339
WILLIAM DITMARS HOUSE
3637 Pine Crescent
c. 1913

This fine red brick Georgian revival house is unusual in Vancouver where romantically inspired arts and crafts and Tudor revival styles were preferred over the classically derived Georgian style. The side gables with central chimney and flat walls are more typical of the Georgian revival than other Shaughnessy examples of the style, such as the G.E. MacDonald House (311).

340
3590 Cypress Street
c. 1914
Some architectural historians make a distinction between Elizabethan and Tudor revival styles, Elizabethan having 'less stonework and less of a fort-like appearance.' The massive granite walls and air of strength and permanence places this house squarely in the Tudor tradition. The decorated entrance and an arcade opening out into the extensive gardens are outstanding features.

341
J.C HAWKINS HOUSE
1927 West 17th Avenue
1912
This unusual residence and the houses at 1938, 1979, and 1995 West 17th Avenue are among the best surviving Queen Anne style homes in the city. No. 1927 features a centrally positioned domed tower, bellcast roofline, and a double-pitched side gable, while the other three houses have the corner turrets and generous porches usually associated with the Queen Anne style.

342
POINT GREY SECONDARY
SCHOOL
5350 East Boulevard
Townley & Matheson 1928-9
The 'dreaming spires' of Oxford and the academic Gothic of Cambridge are the images evoked by this Gothic revival school with its octagonal towers, shields and quatrefoils, and blind lancet arches. This is a fine example of the artistic possibilities of poured-in-place concrete that were explored by architects in the late 1920s and early 1930s.

*West Side whimsy comes in
many forms. Château style enjoyed
a brief reign between the wars.*

4200-block West 10th Avenue

Area Nine **THE WEST SIDE**

A GLANCE at the map reveals that the principal land mass of Vancouver is a large peninsula that terminates to the west at Point Grey. The first Europeans to sight the sandy cliffs of Point Grey were the crew of Commander Narváez who investigated the Strait of Georgia for Spain in 1791. Captain George Vancouver explored the area the following year and named the point after his colleague, Captain George Grey.

Two-thirds of a century passed before Europeans showed further interest in the peninsula. In 1859 land was surveyed and reserved at the end of Point Grey and at Jericho for naval and military purposes. At about the same time, farmers began to settle along the north arm of the Fraser River and in the 1870s a modest agricultural community developed around the farmhouse of Samuel and Fitzgerald McCleery (demolished 1956 for a public golf course).

When land from English Bay to 16th Avenue was incorporated into Vancouver in 1886, the sawmills soon yielded to housing. The area known as Kitsilano developed rapidly after 1909 with the completion of the second Granville Bridge and the extension of streetcar lines. It was

an early 'streetcar suburb' whose rows of developer-built housing offered a less expensive alternative to the West End. The first large-scale project was Talton Place (1910-14), on the 1900- and 2000-blocks of West 13th to 16th avenues, with its 'craftsman bungalows,' factory-built in Vancouver and reassembled on ample 50-foot lots.

The West Side was populated chiefly by the economically and politically dominant professionals and managers who had originally settled in the West End. Much of the territory comprised the CPR's immense District Lot 526. The CPR controlled the rate of development, ensuring orderly growth and maintaining a uniform level of quality.

In 1906 the area west of Ontario Street and south of 16th Avenue separated from the District of South Vancouver. Two years later this breakaway district was incorporated as the Municipality of Point Grey. An upper-income suburb from the start, Point Grey's healthy tax base was given a boost by the development of Shaughnessy Heights within its borders. Citizens consistently voted for municipal improvements, and in 1922 Point Grey enacted the first zoning by-law in Canada, with

left: 'Shannon,' one of the city's grandest mansions, is set in an Italianate garden.

right: Modern homes in older neighbour-hoods (a sensitive issue on the West Side) need not be slavish copies of the past. 'Seascapes' is scaled to its surroundings but refreshingly modern in its response.

controls that differentiated between residential and commercial areas. As a consequence, the area boasts uniform tree-lined streets, planted boulevards, and many parks. The principal shopping district became Kerrisdale, along 41st Avenue.

Point Grey and working-class South Vancouver were reunited when they were absorbed into the City of Vancouver in 1927. A new City Hall was built on Cambie Street as a symbol of amalgamation. Despite the supposed equalization of services, the original physical and economic differences are still evident.

Recent planning has permitted densification, while encouraging new design that recalls traditional architectural forms and pays only lip service to heritage conservation. The outcome has been infill dwellings on narrow lots, 'monster' houses, multi-family housing that compresses a multitude of units into low-rise blocks, and new duplexes that are barely distinguishable from the single-family houses they have replaced. The West Side is changing quickly, and time will tell whether or not for the better.

343
VANCOUVER MUSEUM & H.R. MacMILLAN PLANETARIUM
1100 Chestnut Street
Gerald Hamilton & Associates
1967-8

The Salish Indians' conical cap inspired the dome of the planetarium. Beneath it is the museum, with its delicate lacework of white precast concrete. Sculptor George Norris's popular *Crab* guards the entrance. Nearby in Vanier Park are the City of Vancouver Archives (by McCarter, Nairne & Partners 1971-2) and Vancouver Academy of Music (by Vladimir Plavsic 1976).

344
VANCOUVER MARITIME MUSEUM
ST. ROCH NATIONAL HISTORIC SITE
1905 Ogden Avenue
Raymond O. Harrison; C.B.K. Van Norman & Associates 1958-66

The 80-ton RCMP Arctic patrol vessel *St. Roch*, built in 1928 and the first boat to conquer the Northwest Passage in both directions, rests inside a shingle-and-glass A-frame shelter. It and the Maritime Museum beside it commemorate the region's colourful and significant maritime past.

345
1854-74 West 1st Avenue
John Hollifield 1985

A few strokes of the designer's pen created an instant pseudo-Toronto kitsch village, built by *Yorkville* Developments. The lower floors – occupied by upmarket shops – are disguised by six pseudo-historic house façades of wood, brick, and stone, embellished with gables, bay windows, and wrought-iron fences. Residential suites fill the set-back upper storeys of this silly pastiche.

346

CANADIAN IMPERIAL BANK OF COMMERCE
2199 West 4th Avenue
1910

Streetcar service along 4th Avenue began in 1908 (two years before Broadway), making it the commercial 'high street' of Kitsilano, which it still is today. The Bank of Commerce responded by building a fine brick and stone neoclassical branch that would look at home as the principal bank on the main street of an isolated prairie town.

347

ARBUTUS GROCERY
2200 Arbutus Street
1908

Corner grocery stores spread through residential neighbourhoods before use-restricting zoning bylaws were adopted. Today, many are operated by Chinese Canadians, who entered the business after dominating truck gardening. Originally the Eureka Grocery, this intact store (with its attached dwelling) features a 'boomtown' false front; another is seen on the building across the street.

348

KITSILANO PRESBYTERIAN SABBATH SCHOOL
1855 Vine Street
1910

A sandstone façade and paired Corinthian columns suggest a gracious Toronto or Montreal townhouse, not a Vancouver Sunday School. This must have looked quite out of place amidst a sea of wood bungalows. The Reverend Peter Wright's school served more recently as a Native Indian centre, and has since been divided into five suites with underground parking.

349
MATTHEW LOGAN HOUSE
2530 Point Grey Road
Honeyman & Curtis 1909-10
Built for businessman Logan, and later the home of newspaper publisher and philanthropist Victor Odlum, this elegant residence stands on a quiet and exclusive extension of Point Grey Road. Superb craftsmanship is evident throughout, in the curved glass of the bow window, the leaded panes, the delicate classical frieze, and the balustrade. The stone wall distances it from the street.

350
SEASCAPES
2405 West 2nd Avenue
Hughes Baldwin 1990
Curved blue balconies and floating roofs lift this award-winning 18-suite apartment building above the ordinary, although its 3-storey grey stucco walls are intentionally left plain to blend in with the area's earlier walk-ups. The building bursts open at the entrance, exposing the doorways to the street and giving the units a sense of identity.

351
2100-block Macdonald Street
Lockie & Miller (builders) 1911
Kitsilano developed as a less expensive suburban alternative to the West End. Endless rows of developer-built houses lined the grid of streets, their gabled roofs picturesque and not boring. Many, as here, resemble West End houses of preceding years, but have the wider proportions, broad verandahs, and wood brackets popularized by the newer and trendier California bungalow.

352

2900-3000-blocks West 5th Avenue
Fred Melton, Cook & Hawkins
(builders) 1919-21

The favourite house in the 1910s and
early 1920s was the California (or craftsman) bungalow, which spread from the
western U.S. in pattern books. The typical bungalow has one storey (or an un-
derstated second floor), a verandah, a
gable or two facing the street, abundant
wood trim, and cobblestone or brick
posts. A long row survives here nearly
intact, some renovated or duplexed.

353

TATLOW COURT
1820 Bayswater Street
Frank Mountain 1927-8

The courtyard apartment – with attached units around a landscaped court
– came by way of California, whose climate encouraged indoor-outdoor living.
This is Vancouver's best example, rendered in the cherished Tudor revival.
Renovated in 1977 (by the Corner
Group), dormers were added to light
the attics. The building and park behind
it are named after founding Park Board
member (and Minister of Finance) R.G.
Tatlow.

354

TOWNHOUSES
3267-93 Point Grey Road
Erickson/Massey 1965

Behind a tall laurel hedge and a screen
wall of old brick are five townhouses
built for clients of differing incomes and
tastes. Each has an individual plan, from a
simple 2-bedroom affair to a 5-bedroom
unit with a swimming pool. Only the
brick posts and wood beams are visible
from the street. This was the area's first
multi-unit development; many have followed since.

355
JAMES McMAHON HOUSE
1631 Dunbar Street
S.W. Hopper (builder) 1912

The north ends of Dunbar and Collingwood streets were developed with particularly large craftsman bungalows, most of which have been divided into suites. This brightly painted one, first occupied by butcher McMahon, is wide enough for two (asymmetrical) gabled dormers. The stone base, stubby verandah posts, exposed rafters, and projecting bays are typical of the style.

356
HASTINGS MILL STORE
1575 Alma Street
c. 1865

The oldest building in Vancouver, erected as the general store for the Hastings Mill, this structure was barged in 1930 to its present site and opened as a delightfully quirky museum by the Native Daughters of BC. The vertical board-and-batten siding is an incorrect restoration; early photos show horizontal siding and a 'boomtown' false front.

357
BROCK HOUSE
3875 Point Grey Road
Maclure & Fox 1912-13

Architects Maclure & Fox exploited the Tudor revival style in gracious residences for the social élite. This beachfront manor is named after geologist (and long-time owner) Reginald Brock. It is now a senior citizens' centre and restaurant (alterations by John Keith-King 1976). Visitors can admire the fine arts and crafts interior, with its tall entrance hall, wood panelling, and leaded windows.

358
DOROTHY GRETCHEN STEEVES MANOR
1985 Wallace Street
John Keith-King 1975

Public housing can look good and offer residents privacy and dignity, as this 200-unit complex clearly shows. The 3-storey building, operated by BC Housing, provides landscaped courtyards between the wings. Grey wood siding and horizontal balconies blend well with the site alongside Jericho Park. Named after an early CCF politician, it was built by the short-lived NDP government of the 1970s.

359
JERICHO YOUTH HOSTEL
1515 Discovery Street
Department of National Defence 1937

Acquired in 1971 by the Canadian Youth Hostels Association, this stucco building began as barracks for the Jericho Air Station, whose seaplanes combatted smugglers in the 1920s and the threat of Japanese attack during the Second World War. Now Jericho Park – a beach and bird sanctuary – 'Jerry's Cove' was named after pioneer logger Jeremiah Rogers, who produced fine spars for sailing ships.

360
HORACE BARBER HOUSE
3846 West 10th Avenue
Ross A. Lort 1936

The 1930s ushered in modernist tendencies that rejected period revival styles. Architect Lort – former partner of arch-traditionalist Samuel Maclure – adopted the austere flat concrete walls (radical for the day), hard edges, and abstract geometry of the moderne style. The house has been rehabilitated and a compatible infill dwelling built at the rear (by Robert G. Lemon 1990).

361
4167 West 11th Avenue
Stuart Howard 1987

This is one of several 'thin houses' in west Point Grey (another is down the block at 4127 West 11th) – a scant 16 feet wide yet well proportioned. The front door opens into the living room, and other rooms are stacked behind. Developers can split 50-foot properties into separate lots of 33 and 16 feet. As infill, thin house can help to preserve residential heritage.

362
THE NEW VANCOUVER
SPECIAL
4360 West 11th Avenue
Stuart Howard 1985

Dissatisfied with the appearance of the Vancouver Special (see 428), the Vancouver League for Studies in Architecture and the Environment sponsored a competition to find a better design. Winner Stuart Howard's prototype features traditional materials, vertical massing, steep roofs, and a semi-detached rear extension, providing the same density in a more attractive package – but it hasn't caught on.

363
JAMES CASHMAN HOUSE
4686 West 2nd Avenue
Perry & Fowler 1919

The 'honest' use of indigenous materials – the rallying cry of the arts and crafts movement – is here carried to an extreme. Logs form the walls and large stones are used for the foundation and chimney of this large but cozy home. Verandahs on both floors provide a view across the park towards the water and mountains. The rustic charm is emphasized by the mature trees.

364
KANIA CASTLE
4585 Bellevue Drive
1935-6

The Spanish colonial revival – with stucco walls, red pantile roofs, arched openings, and wrought-iron balconies – swept California in the 1920s and drifted north to BC. This house, built for broker Joseph Kania and perched high on a steep escarpment, is an example of this style. The once-white walls are painted, with glorious historical inaccuracy, in vivid salmon pink.

365
RIDGE THEATRE
3131 Arbutus Street
Kaplan & Sprachman 1949-50

A modern variant of the 1920s picture palace, the narrow foyer opens to the street in a tall, theatrical bay filled by a billboard-sized stained-glass window and topped by expressive, free-standing typography. The 800-seat theatre is part of a small (and early) strip mall, whose bowling alley is advertised by an enormous roof-top bowling pin.

366
STEFANOPOULOS HOUSE
2172 West 16th Avenue
Rallis Building Design 1986

The 'monster house,' to many people an alarming phenomenon that began in the 1980s, has taken over large areas of the West Side. This isolated example looks particularly out of scale among its much smaller neighbours. The bow of Corinthian columns shamelessly plagiarizes the White House. The peculiar brand of neoclassicism is emphasized by the balustrade-like fence.

367
ST. GEORGE'S GREEK ORTHODOX CATHEDRAL
4500 Arbutus Street
Hamilton, Doyle & Associates
1970-1

Delicate arches and patterned screen walls of precast concrete are capped by a shallow dome in a characteristic example of the neoclassicism seen in the short-lived 'new formalist' style. The cathedral serves the city's large Greek-Canadian population, whose main commercial district is located along Broadway near Macdonald Street.

368
BOWSER BLOCK
5729 West Boulevard
1912

Kerrisdale was Point Grey's civic and commercial centre, with a stop on the interurban railway and the former Point Grey municipal hall a block south on 42nd Avenue (now occupied by the library and community centre). Local booster Francis Bowser built this pioneer commercial block. A number of low 1910s and 1920s shops along 41st Avenue, intermingled with newer buildings, serve the upmarket retail trade.

369
ST. MARY'S, KERRISDALE
2498 West 37th Avenue
Sharp & Thompson 1913

Architects Sharp & Thompson evoked the spirit of their native England in this Anglican parish church, although with shingled and board-and-batten walls that exploit BC wood. The interior glows from the marvellous stained glass and brass lanterns. Additions to either end (by Twizell and Twizell 1947) retained the character. Sharp's own fine house (1912) is across the street at No. 2427.

370

CONVENT OF THE SACRED HEART
3851 West 29th Avenue
Charles G. Badgley 1912

This imposing granite-faced building has housed the junior division of St. George's School (371) since 1978. The central tower (with drive-through porte-cochère) and the broad wings are treated in a castellated version of the Gothic revival once popular for religious and educational buildings. The plain brick rear forms a nice contrast, as does the brick gatekeeper's cottage.

371

ST. GEORGE'S SCHOOL
4175 West 29th Avenue
Mark Sharp 1965

Founded in 1931 as a private boys' school, St. George's is respected for upholding traditional values. This is expressed in the junior school (370), but the senior school makes a more modernist statement, reinterpreting the prairie style of Frank Lloyd Wright with ground-hugging lines and warm materials – wood siding, laminated wood beams, reddish concrete block, and copper roofs.

372

DON MacFARLAND HOUSE
6290 Collingwood Street
Dalla-Lana/Griffin 1977

Fred Dalla-Lana (who trained with Arthur Erickson) was one of a group of talented architects who emerged in the 1970s and 1980s. They updated the post-and-beam theme with aggressive compositions that challenged the balance seen in earlier work (contrast 527). Here the stone chimney and penthouse bulges counter the horizontality of the lower floors in a masterly composition.

373
GOLDEN OAK STABLES
7376 Blenheim Street
Stuart Howard 1989-90

Below SW Marine Drive the ground drops quickly to the Southlands, fertile land farmed by the McCleerys, Magees, and Moles before there was a Vancouver. The farms and market gardens have gone, but the flats remain a semi-rural equestrian and gardening centre. Golden Oak is one of many stables. The houses, barn, and outbuildings, pleasingly designed by Maura Gatensby, recall farm architecture.

374
CELTIC SHIPYARDS
3150 Celtic Avenue
Ward & Sons Construction 1941

Working and recreational boats are repaired and built at this shipyard, which occupies a group of frame structures built as the provincial Forest Service Marine Station and now owned by the Musqueam Band. 'Celtic' was the name of the nearby shipyard that serviced part of the BC Packers fishing fleet, later consolidated with other facilities at Steveston.

375
RIO VISTA
2170 Southwest Marine Drive
Bernard Palmer 1930-1

Harry F. Reifel, son of brewer and distiller Henry Reifel, built the most sumptuous local example of the Spanish colonial revival, complete with an immense conservatory and 'Pompeiian' pool. His brother George erected Casa Mia nearby (1920 SW Marine Drive; by Ross A. Lort 1932). Local mythology hints that both launched bootlegging operations from the Fraser River flats below their houses.

376
SAFEWAY STORE
8555 Granville Street
Frank Roy 1966

Canada Safeway Limited built a number of supermarkets with this distinctive design – a sweeping double-curved roof defined by arched glued-laminated ('glulam') beams and supported inside by only a few pipe columns. The glass façade is flanked by fieldstone walls. This is one of few stores that remain unchanged (contrast with the Safeway at 2300 West 4th, altered 1992).

377
SHANNON MEWS
7101-201 Granville Street
Somervell & Putnam 1915-25,
Arthur Erickson 1972-3

The 10-acre Shannon estate, with a grand brick and stone Georgian revival mansion and the city's best Italianate landscape garden, was built for sugar king B.T. Rogers (see 70). Financier Austin Taylor subsequently lived here. The house, formal gardens, gatehouse, and coachhouse survive in restored splendour amidst a bevy of exquisitely designed and discretely sited luxury townhouses and apartments.

378
GRANVILLE CHAPEL
5901 Granville Street
Robert R. McKee 1949-50

International modernism reached the city's religious architecture in this austerely rectilinear gospel hall built for the Plymouth Brethren. A tall corner tower (the only church-like feature) contrasts with otherwise horizontal lines. Steel beams span the 600-seat central auditorium, whose clerestory windows peek over the façade; otherwise the structure is wood, covered with a veneer of thin red bricks.

379
WILLIAM H. JAMES HOUSE
**587 West King Edward Avenue
1941**

A cozy Cotswold cottage was the model for this quaint residence. The undulating shingle roof imitates thatching; and half-timbering, rubble stonework, and stucco complete the fairy-tale imagery. Builder Brenton T. Lea built several speculative houses like this. Others are at 3979 West Broadway and in West Vancouver (506). Architect Ross A. Lort may have provided the design.

380
BETH ISRAEL SYNAGOGUE
**4350 Oak Street
Kaplan & Sprachman 1948**

The focus of Vancouver's Jewish community shifted southward from Strathcona (see 61) to the Oak Street and Oakridge areas. Imposing Beth Israel has a classically symmetrical composition expressed with sleek modernist presence. Vancouver Talmud Torah School (begun 1947), across 27th Avenue, is similarly designed, although with rough exposed concrete.

381
CHILDREN'S HOSPITAL
**4480 Oak Street
Gardiner Thornton Partnership
1981-2**

Many of the city's health-care facilities are located here. Children's Hospital and the Salvation Army's Grace Hospital share this concrete and metal-sided building. The rest of the site accommodates University (formerly Shaughnessy) Hospital (382), with the Canadian Red Cross a stone's throw away, and Vancouver General (291-3) and St. Vincent's Hospital nearby. The colour scheme reduces the building's austerity.

382
JEAN MATHESON MEMORIAL PAVILION
University Hospital
4500 Oak Street
Mercer & Mercer 1946

University Hospital was formed in 1988 with the merger of Shaughnessy Hospital and the UBC Health Sciences Centre Hospital. This Shaughnessy site has a number of good 1930s and 1940s buildings. The Matheson Pavilion's moderne entrance features vestigial fluted shafts, period lettering, and red vitrolite (a glass product). The other side is even better.

383
UNITY CHURCH OF TODAY
5840 Oak Street
W.D. Buttjes 1964

The whale-like profile of the curved roof beams provides this non-mainstream church with a distinctive image. This stretch of Oak Street has attracted many religious institutions outside of established denominations, including the Chinese Seventh-Day Adventist Church and the Kabalarian Philosophy just to the south, and the Lubavitch Centre next door to the north; each of these buildings is striking in its own way.

384
UNITARIAN CHURCH OF VANCOUVER
949 West 49th Avenue
Wolfgang Gerson, with R. Hale 1964

This handsome building avoids the clichés of church design to disassociate the Unitarian Church from mainstream Christianity. Three buildings are grouped around an open court: the tall sanctuary at the north, the school to the west, and the administration block at the corner. Contrast the traditional steep roofs and spire of the Estonian Lutheran Church of St. Peter (1964) across the street.

385
VANCOUVER COMMUNITY COLLEGE, LANGARA
100 West 49th Avenue
Ronald B. Howard, with Allan B. Wilson 1969-70

This municipal college was built on part of the CPR's Langara Golf Course. The complex has a tall library block and lower academic and gymnasium blocks, all warmly finished in textured concrete and red brick. Additions were made in the 1980s by Downs/Archambault. It reflects the movement away from the disciplined international style towards brutalism.

386
TEMPLE SHOLOM
7190 Oak Street
Henriquez & Partners 1986-7

Warm red concrete block, a generous setback, and fine landscaping give this Reformed Jewish synagogue a friendly, domestic look that provides a sense of ceremony without solemn clichés. The bowed entrance and shallow copper dome are foils to the angular bay windows. Next door, the brick townhouses of Cobble Lane (by Raymond Letkeman 1992) pay homage to the temple.

387
JAMES RAMSAY HOUSE
1196 West 59th Avenue
1912

This superb Queen Anne house, with its gracious columned verandah and porte-cochère, was the home of chocolate manufacturer and politician James Ramsay. The once enormous property has been subdivided, but the garden, gazebo, and stone wall remain. The house has served as a child welfare facility for more than fifty years.

388
VANCOUVER SOUTH TRANSFER STATION
377 West Kent Ave North
Bush, Bohlman & Partners
(engineers) 1988

As recycling becomes a priority, the importance of this municipal facility is ever more evident. Plastics, newspaper, metals, and used appliances are sorted in this massive concrete bunker, where they are forwarded to recyclers, while garbage is sent to the landfill at Burns Bog. A landscaped berm partially conceals the structure.

389
DOMAN FOREST PRODUCTS SAWMILL
West Kent Avenue North at
Heather Street
largely rebuilt by Stolberg
Engineering 1985-6

The Fraser River once fed lumber to a long line of sawmills, several of which remain. The corrugated-metal sheds of the Doman complex (operating since the 1920s) respond to the mill's functions. Other mills include Mitchell Island Forest Products beside it, Mainland Sawmills at the foot of Yukon, and the Canfor mill at Milton and West 75th Avenue.

390
CHRYSLER CANADA PARTS DISTRIBUTION CENTRE
26 Southwest Marine Drive
McCarter & Nairne 1956

This sublimely simple building offers an elegant statement of Bauhaus-inspired modernist ideals. The formal office façade, set well back on the lawn, features a stone entrance, bands of windows, aluminum lettering, and a red brick wall. The rear elevation – the 'working' warehouse side – is fully glazed and exposes the steel structural frame.

A magnificent building,

responsive to its setting

and the culture it celebrates

Museum of Anthropology

**UNIVERSITY OF
BRITISH
COLUMBIA**

T HE University of British Columbia was created by provincial legislation in 1908. A magnificent 260-acre site was selected at the tip
of Point Grey, and in 1912 a competition was held to solicit a design for
the new campus. The architectural assessors were fond of traditional
British design, and their unanimous choice was the partnership of
George L.T. Sharp and Charles J. Thompson, two young English architects, recently arrived in Canada.

The architects' grandly scaled plan for the campus applied formal
beaux-arts planning principles to the scenic site; they proposed that the
administration occupy the highest elevation at University Boulevard and
Main Mall, and assigned each faculty to its own precinct. A hierarchy of
academic values was embedded in the plan, with the most central site
reserved for science, the southern portion for agriculture, and the periphery for theology, athletics, and the military.

The buildings were designed in the collegiate Gothic style, de-
scribed by the architects as 'a free rendering of Modern Tudor' that
clearly recalled the hallowed walls of Oxford and Cambridge. Con-

struction began in 1914, but the First World War and the death of UBC president Frank Wesbrook brought work to a halt. It took the Great Trek of 1922, in which students marched from the temporary Fairview campus to the Point Grey site, to remind the government of its commitment. The new campus opened for classes in the fall of 1925.

The Science (now Chemistry) Building and the central portion of the Main Library were the only structures to be completed to the high standards of design and finishes specified by Sharp & Thompson, with stone walls on a reinforced concrete structure. Subsequent buildings used cheaper wood-frame construction and a stucco finish.

After the Second World War, the campus architects – by now Sharp & Thompson, Berwick, Pratt – introduced the modernist international style. Early landmarks are the War Memorial Gymnasium and the Buchanan Building. Expansion was steady through the 1960, with other architectural firms broadening the range of styles and approaches. A large infusion of capital funds in the 1980s, much of it from Asian-Canadian philanthropists, has produced a new building boom. A

left: *The Asian Centre, a serene building beautifully set on UBC's leafy campus*

right: *French provincial, Scottish baronial, and Tudor revival blend in this villa (on Western Crescent), one of many varied homes on the University Endowment Lands.*

campus plan produced in 1991 by duToit, Allsopp, Hillier recognized the need to accommodate growth while respecting the grid, sightlines, and values expressed by the Sharp & Thompson plan.

A key feature of the original provincial land grant was the establishment of the University Endowment Lands (UEL) as a buffer between UBC and Vancouver. It had been anticipated that the university would draw income from the large property, but the UEL was developed instead as an upper-income residential community with its own municipal government. A number of fine houses grace the area.

Several changes to the UEL and UBC came about in the 1980s. Some 1,855 acres of undeveloped forests, bluffs, and beaches were ceded to the Greater Vancouver Regional District, and renamed Pacific Spirit Regional Park. UBC set aside a large tract on the southeast corner of campus as Discovery Park, a centre for scientific and industrial research. And a 28-acre portion between Discovery Park and the main campus is being transformed by UBC Real Estate Corporation into a dense residential housing development called Hampton Place.

391
CHEMISTRY BUILDING
2036 Main Mall, UBC
Sharp & Thompson 1914-25
Originally the Science Building, this was the first structure on the campus, and the only completed as planned, with stone walls in the collegiate Gothic style. Its strong character has withstood the onslaught of several contrasting additions (by Thompson, Berwick & Pratt). Later campus buildings, such as the Old Auditorium (6344 Memorial Road), were rendered in stucco with only vague Gothic allusions.

392
MAIN LIBRARY
1956 Main Mall, UBC
Sharp & Thompson 1923-5
The central portion of the library, like the Chemistry Building, features stone walls and Gothic detail, but the later wings (1947-8, 1959-60) are more cheaply finished in stucco (as were other campus buildings). Two skylights on the treed Main Mall, and a deep forecourt, illuminate the Sedgewick Undergraduate Library (by Rhone & Iredale 1971-2), soon to be obliterated by a large new addition.

393
BUCHANAN BUILDING
1866 Main Mall, UBC
Thompson, Berwick & Pratt
1956-8, 1960
A new building program begun in the 1950s introduced the modernist international style to the UBC campus. The Buchanan Building has precise, rectilinear walls of grey glazed brick, painted concrete, enamel panels, and glass. The tower (by Toby, Russell, Buckwell & Associates 1970-2) offers a later, more brutalist, touch.

394
DAVID LAM MANAGEMENT RESEARCH CENTRE
2033 Main Mall, UBC
CJP Architects 1992

The architectural diversity along this historic portion of Main Mall has been enhanced by this extension to the business school, endowed and named after Hong Kong-born industrialist and lieutenant governor, David Lam. Separate wings of concrete, glass, and brick – the central one a glazed stairwell and atrium – pay homage to nearly all of the styles and materials in the vicinity.

395
FIRST NATIONS HOUSE OF LEARNING
1985 West Mall, UBC
Larry McFarland 1991-2

Inspired by the longhouses of the Coast Salish, this impressive structure is a meeting place and support facility for First Nations students. The 3,000-square-foot Great Hall features carved house posts supporting massive 3-foot roof beams. Compare the modern replicas of longhouses behind the Museum of Anthropology (403) and the museum itself, which were inspired by the same source.

396
ASIAN CENTRE
1871 West Mall, UBC
Donald Matsuba 1981

Like an oversized lid, a broad, pyramidal, hipped metal roof covers this serene building, its steel beams reused from a pavilion at Expo in Osaka. A moat-like reflecting pool encircles it. The centre contains the Department of Asian Studies, its library, a gallery, and an auditorium. A traditional Japanese bell tower stands beside it, and the lovely Nitobe Memorial Gardens are situated behind.

397
GEOLOGICAL SCIENCES BUILDING
6339 Stores Road, UBC
McCarter, Nairne & Partners 1971
Sleek vertical panels of white porcelain enamel and dark glass in an abstract de Stijl-like pattern mark the main block, separated from the more classically composed south wing by a glazed stairwell link. Multi-coloured round ventilator shafts add a decorative touch. The ensemble is a timeless update of the Bauhaus manner. An outdoor mineral display advertises the M.Y. Williams Geological Museum.

398
H.R. MacMILLAN BUILDING
2357 Main Mall, UBC
McCarter, Nairne & Partners 1967
Forestry and Agriculture share a superb reinterpretation of collegiate Gothic, enlivened with a soupçon of Frank Lloyd Wright. Arranged around a lovely landscaped quadrangle, entered through a post-and-beam gate, the red brick building (with white concrete bands) has vertical buttress-like piers between the windows. The Frank A. Forward Building nearby, completed by the same architects (1968), continues the theme.

399
WAR MEMORIAL GYMNASIUM
6081 University Boulevard, UBC
Sharp & Thompson, Berwick, Pratt 1951
This simple, cubic university gymnasium was UBC's first modern building. Consulting architect Professor Frederick Lasserre and engineer F.W. Urry helped conceive the massive structural roof truss that projects downward into the gym, avoiding the need for columns without interrupting sight lines. The adjacent Empire Pool was built for the 1954 Empire Games.

400
P.A. WOODWARD INSTRUC-
TIONAL RESOURCES CENTRE
2194 Health Sciences Mall, UBC
Thompson, Berwick, Pratt &
Partners 1970-2

Raw reinforced concrete – with form-holes left unfilled – is seen here at its brutalist best, the top floor a heavy cornice-like cantilevered slab and three bold staircase towers projecting from the rear (south) elevation. The IRC is set amidst a sea of health-sciences buildings (supporting UBC's excellent medical school) in this, the most urban street-scape on the UBC campus.

401
FOREST ENGINEERING
RESEARCH INSTITUTE OF
CANADA
2601 East Mall, UBC
Henry Hawthorn 1989-90

Wood is exploited here in a delightfully picturesque way. The building seems to float within the exposed bolted frame which consists of laminated posts and beams with western red cedar siding. The recessed central entrance is flanked by asymmetrical angled glass pavilions in a dynamic composition.

402
HAMPTON PLACE
off Wesbrook Mall
begun 1990

UBC Real Estate Corporation is developing a 28-acre tract with more than 700 townhouse and apartment units, whose names and style provide a pastiche of olde England. Thames Court (by Howard/Yano 1990-2) and West Hampstead (by Larry Laidlaw 1992) are born-again Tudor revival, one in brick and half-timber, the other in wood.

403
MUSEUM OF ANTHROPOLOGY
6393 Northwest Marine Drive, UBC
Arthur Erickson 1973-6

Muscular concrete posts supporting broad beams (inspired by the coastal Natives' cedar houses) frame this spectacular museum on a magnificent cliffside site. The floor slopes down from the entrance and the ceiling rises to create a dramatic and spacious setting for huge totem poles and house frames. The museum expanded its scope and size with the Koerner Ceramics Gallery (by Erickson 1990).

404
POINT GREY BATTERY
foot of Cecil Green Park Road
Department of National Defence 1939

During the Second World War, defences were erected along the BC coast to resist possible Japanese attack. This concrete platform supported a 6-inch artillery gun with an 8-mile range. Ammunition was stored in the magazine beneath. Targets could be illuminated by searchlight emplacements on the shore below; they survive as curiosities on Wreck Beach, Vancouver's nude beach.

405
CECIL GREEN PARK
6251 Cecil Green Park Road, UBC
Maclure & Fox 1911

Built by lawyer E.P. Davis, this arts and crafts-cum-Tudor revival mansion was bought in 1966 by UBC alumnus Dr. Cecil Green and donated to the university as a social and alumni facility. The grounds and interior, with a galleried hall and splendid woodwork, deserve a visit. The Lefevre-Graham house next door (by Maclure & Fox 1915) will soon form the nucleus of Green College (by Paul Merrick, begun 1992).

406
CANTERBURY HOUSE
Vancouver School of Theology
6090 Chancellor Boulevard
1927

This superb Voyseyesque arts and crafts stucco block was erected for the Anglican Theological College. It and the rubble-stone Chapel of the Epiphany (by David Hickman 1966) now form part of the Vancouver School of Theology after a 1971 amalgamation with the United Church's Union College. See also the large Iona Building (by Sharp & Thompson 1927).

407
JOHN G. BENNETT HOUSE
6035 Newton Wynd
Thompson, Berwick & Pratt 1953

Ron Thom, a doyen of the West Coast style (also famed for public projects like Massey College, Toronto), designed this superb Point Grey house overlooking NW Marine Drive. A masterly composition, its horizontal emphasis, wide eaves, form, and massing recall Frank Lloyd Wright, whose style the client favoured. Unusually (for Thom) lavish materials — Vermont slate, African hardwood, and Arizona sandstone — are used throughout.

408
DOUGLAS SIMPSON & HAROLD SEMMENS HOUSES
4862-72 Queensland Drive
Semmens & Simpson 1949

Architects Doug Simpson and Hal Semmens began a Vancouver practice in the late 1940s and quickly became the city's brashest and most committed modernists. Their clean, non-historicist forms rendered in local materials are evident in these side-by-side residences in the UEL's 'little Australia,' a former training ground for Aussie troops.

A Mediterranean piazza

on Slocan Street

Italian Cultural Centre

Area Eleven　**SOUTH VANCOUVER**

THE District of South Vancouver, organized in 1892, comprised the vast area between 16th Avenue and the Fraser River, from the Strait of Georgia east to today's Boundary Road. It contained a number of rural-suburban neighbourhoods linked to Vancouver and New Westminster by the interurban railway. The majority of residents were British working-class folk whose first priority was keeping taxes down. For more than a dozen years, the municipality refused to issue debentures to finance improvements. Roads often followed the construction of housing. This laissez-faire atmosphere drove frustrated West Side residents to secede and form the Municipality of Point Grey in 1906.

South Vancouver's promoters championed the western Canadian ideal of every family having a detached house with a garden. Small houses became the norm. The lack of municipal planning controls allowed a variety of lot sizes and setbacks and a paucity of street trees. South Vancouver was never properly surveyed and had no integrated plan. Streets are narrow and poorly aligned, residential areas often contain commercial and industrial uses, and few parks were deliberately

left: *A 'Vancouver Special' at Elgin and Ross streets.*

right: *Contemporary builder's styles display fey and, at times, outrageous historicism (600-block East 18th Avenue).*

planned. Some areas developed much like a patchwork quilt, containing houses from several eras and of contrasting sizes along a single block. South Vancouver and Point Grey were amalgamated into the City of Vancouver in 1927, but the contrast between the two areas remains. The haphazard appearance of the East Side differs considerably from the uniformity of the West Side. The designation 'East' and 'West' on the city's streets provide a constant reminder of the divisions.

Families of British origin no longer dominate the area that was South Vancouver. Since the Second World War, the East Side has become home to many ethnic communities. Several have developed distinctive commercial districts. The retail stores and social institutions of the Italian community were concentrated along Commercial Drive, those of the East Indians along Victoria Drive, south of 41st Avenue. Large numbers of Chinese Canadians have established roots throughout the area, far beyond the boundaries of Chinatown.

The past few decades have brought many architectural, as well as demographic, changes to South Vancouver. The 1970s introduced a

new cost-effective, but unattractive, house type called the 'Vancouver Special.' Developers assembled large tracts of land and filled them with rows upon rows of these bland single-family and duplex houses.

Several large-scale, government-planned (but privately built) developments have occurred since the Second World War. Fraserview was filled with modest single-family housing for returning veterans. To the southeast, Champlain Heights – the last undeveloped track of land in the city – was developed by the city in the 1970s and 1980s as a model residential community, with a dense mix of assisted and market multi-family housing. The most recent initiative, also by the city, has been the development of the Fraser Lands, the area along the north shore of the Fraser River between the Knight Street Bridge and the boundary with Burnaby. By 1996 the former industrial area will be transformed into a residential community with 2,600 dwelling units, mostly low-rise townhouses but with a smattering of high rises. Once the Fraser Lands have been filled, future densification can occur only with the redevelopment (or infill) of existing residential neighbourhoods.

409
WALDEN BUILDING
4120 Main Street
1911

Many had high hopes that Main Street would live up to its name, but the few substantial structures south of Mt. Pleasant remain isolated. The 3-storey Walden Building flaunts a dignified brick façade, the other sides cheaply finished in stucco and wood. The adjacent block and one across the street are in similar scale, but the corner is otherwise dominated by gas stations and a strip mall.

410
300-block East 28th Avenue
Various builders and dates

The development of South Vancouver was far less consistent than Point Grey. This block contains 15 houses (one a former corner store), mostly unrelated in design. Two are new Vancouver Specials; the rest were built around the First World War. Unlike Point Grey's uniform 24-foot setback, several are 10 feet or less from the sidewalk, leaving large rear yards for gardens.

411
LITTLE MOUNTAIN PUBLIC HOUSING
33rd to 37th avenues, between Ontario & Main
Thompson, Berwick & Pratt 1952-3

Inspired by postwar idealism, but characterized by blandness, Vancouver's first low-rental housing project contains 224 units of row-type housing and apartments. The blocks have flat roofs and pale yellow stucco walls. More recent developments of this type are better designed and try to integrate the residents into the community.

412
NAT BAILEY STADIUM
4601 Ontario Street
1946
This perfect little ballpark, with 6,500 seats, is well supported by loyal fans of Vancouver's Triple-A baseball team, the Canadians. Built and donated to the city by Sick's Capilano Brewery, and called Capilano Stadium, it was later owned by Molson's, which renamed the team after its beer. Nat Bailey, who founded the White Spot restaurant chain, was an ardent baseball fan who sponsored the team during lean years.

413
BLOEDEL CONSERVATORY
Queen Elizabeth Park
Underwood, McKinley, Cameron,
Wilson & Smith 1969
Tropical plants and chattering birds thrive beneath the 'triodetic' dome, 140 feet in diameter, assembled from aluminum pipe and plexiglas bubbles (by Thorson & Thorson, structural engineers). The same architects designed the adjacent restaurant (1972-3). The structures crown 500-foot-high Little Mountain, the highest point in the city. Below, two abandoned basalt quarries have been transformed into marvellous gardens.

414
CHURCH OF THE GOOD SHEPHERD
808 East 19th Avenue
E. Egsgaard & A. Jesperson 1937
The curious crow-stepped gable atop the façade – something between a false front and a tower – was built by Danish Lutherans who wanted a reminder of the architecture of their native country. The stepped feature is repeated on the projections at the rear. These symbolic components are placed on an otherwise plain gabled form, finished in local white stucco.

415
ST. MARK'S LUTHERAN CHURCH
1553 East 18th Avenue
1911

Originally the Robson Memorial Methodist Church, this handsome stucco and half-timber church (the shingles have gone from the lower walls) is perched on the crest of a hill. This Cedar Cottage district, named after a farm in the area, was a stop on the tram from Vancouver to New Westminster. The hill and nearby Trout Lake (now John Hendry Park) attracted well-to-do homeowners, but most of the fine homes have gone.

416
ST. JOSEPH'S ROMAN CATHOLIC CHURCH
1612 East 18th Avenue
Harry LeBlond & Associates 1982

The distinction between walls and roofs is obscured in this spirited church, whose sloping sides (supported by glued-laminated rafters) are gently curved in a tent-like form. They do not quite meet at the top, allowing the dramatic entry of light from the apex – a device seen in some Quebec churches of the day. This bold exaggeration of the modernist vocabulary is characteristic of late modernism.

417
VANCOUVER TECHNICAL SCHOOL
2600 East Broadway
Townley & Matheson 1928

More than 2,200 students attend Vancouver Tech, which began as a boys' technical school, admitted girls in 1941 (when a new classroom wing was built), and amalgamated with Grandview High School of Commerce in 1950 (when it was expanded, by E.D. King). The most interesting portions are the somewhat Gothic façade and the factory-like wing at the rear, with its serrated monitor roof.

418
ST. JUDE'S SHRINE
3078 Renfrew Street
Toby, Russell & Buckwell 1964

The folded planes of the roof float above red brick walls in an effective modern interpretation of Gothic vaulting. The large triangular clerestory windows allow light to flood the broad wood-panelled nave. The church is a shrine to St. Jude Thaddeus while also serving a local parish. The brick school to the east was built in 1955.

419
FIRE HALL NO. 15
3003 East 22nd Avenue
1914

Several fire halls were built to this design, notable for its broad hipped roof and craftsman detail. The walls have been stuccoed, but original shingles remain on the tall hose tower and inside the former porch over the doors. To the west are Renfrew Park, with a community centre, and Renfrew Ravine Park, with its rugged setting astride Still Creek, which flows into Burnaby Lake.

420
EARLES STATION
4590 Earles Street
1912

This was the last remaining electrical substation that powered the BC Electric interurban railway, whose right-of-way now accommodates SkyTrain tracks. The massive concrete structure, a landmark in a neighbourhood of bland, low buildings, was superbly converted by Linda Baker (1989) into 12 suites (4 per floor) with the changes, such as the steel balconies, respectful of the original design.

421
2400 MOTEL
2400 Kingsway
1946-7
A rare, unaltered period piece, from the tall neon sign to the immaculate lawns, this 'motor court' offers 65 units in 19 detached cottages spread over 3½ acres. White stucco, green siding, and hipped roofs provide a domestic look, while the flat-roofed office is a more modernistic, commercial affair. The Kingsway, the historic route from New Westminster to Vancouver, was once a motel strip.

422
COLLINGWOOD BRANCH LIBRARY
2985 Kingsway
Semmens & Simpson 1950
One of the first suburban branches of the Vancouver Public Library, and the oldest to survive unaltered, Collingwood demonstrates the use of modern forms to produce a regional West Coast style. The rectilinearity and industrial products (including mass-produced steel-sash windows from England) are tempered by large expanses of glass, rough fieldstone, and brown-stained wood that respond to the local climate and materials.

423
CARLETON SCHOOL
3250 Kingsway
begun 1905
South Vancouver's rapid growth before the First World War is evident in this cluster of school buildings. A one-room schoolhouse (1905) and a two-room annex (1907) at McKinnon Street were eclipsed by the sturdy yellow frame school (by W.T. Whiteway 1908) and the large classical red brick building (by J.H. Bowman 1911-12) – types that reappear in schools across the city. A gymnasium wing (1949) completes the complex.

424
AVALON DAIRY
5805 Wales Street
1906
British Columbia's oldest continuously operating dairy outlet bottles and sells milk in traditional glass bottles. (Avalon products are also available at supermarkets and by home delivery.) The dairy has been owned since 1906 by the Crowley family. The farmhouse is a rare reminder of the city's agricultural past, and still stands in what, deceptively, appears to be a rural setting.

425
CORPUS CHRISTI CHURCH
6350 Nanaimo Street
W.R. Ussner 1962
Sculptor Jack Harman's 16-foot-high welded bronze apostles and Christ with angels rise above the ironstone arcades on the side and front of this assertive church. A scalloped dome marks the narthex. The bright and serene basilica-like interior features relief murals by Harman. A gym, rectory, and other buildings to the north serve this active parish, which was founded by the Oblate Fathers.

426
VALUE VILLAGE
6415 Victoria Drive
McKee & Gray 1960
Now a general discount outlet, this was originally one of many similar supermarkets in the Super-Valu chain. The large glued-laminated timber arches provide a broad interior space entirely uninterrupted by columns, in contrast to those of rival Safeway (376). The astonishingly small metal connectors located where the arches meet the ground bear the full weight of the structure.

427
VANCOUVER HEALTH DEPARTMENT, SOUTH UNIT
6405-45 Knight Street
Duncan McNab & Associates 1960
International style architecture had been considered radical for public building in 1950; a decade later it was the preferred mode. This district health office maintains a comfortably human scale. Exposed steel columns divide the glass and brick infill into small units. The lower entrance leads to a landscaped courtyard.

428
VANCOUVER SPECIALS
6100 & 6200-blocks Elgin & Ross streets
Various builders 1970s-80s
Around 1970, builders found a new model for mass-market housing that maximized floor area and site coverage at an attractive price. The 'Vancouver Specials' are unique in that they quickly achieved widespread unpopularity for their boring flat fronts, boxy shapes, and low roofs. These adjacent blocks offer wide variety in the ersatz materials, pastel colours, and entrance details.

429
MEMORIAL PARK SOUTH FIELD HOUSE
near East 41st Avenue & Windsor Street
c. 1932
Dedicated in 1927, Memorial Park South features a grand boulevard entrance from 41st Avenue and fine stands of trees. The picturesque field house was built shortly after amalgamation with Vancouver. The rustic structure has board-and-batten siding, a steep roof whose broad eaves are supported by posts, and attractive woodwork in the gables.

430
6288 Windsor Street
Henry Whittaker 1919
This dilapidated, but unaltered, mansard-roofed Dutch colonial dwelling was one of ten in the area built by the provincial Department of Lands under the federal Better Housing Scheme to provide affordable housing for veterans and widows of the First World War. Another is at 6273 Windsor. All cost $2,500 or less. In all, 153 houses were built or improved in Vancouver over five years.

431
POPE HOUSE
6306 Prince Albert Street
1912
This precious red and yellow frame house, first occupied by fireman Ennis Pope, features a delightful octagonal corner verandah with a ball finial at the peak of its conical roof, transforming a cottage into a toytown château. The entrance is set at an angle, and leaded glass graces many of the windows. The property is attractively landscaped and the house immaculately maintained.

432
UNIVERSAL BUDDHIST TEMPLE
525 East 49th Avenue
Vincent Kwan 1978
The temple was founded by C.C. Lu in 1968 to serve a group of lay Buddhists. The colourful cubic building, built a decade later, is finished in pink stucco with red columns, and capped by a characteristically Chinese two-tiered gold tiled roof featuring a pair of serpents and a ball on the ridge. Ceramic tiles below the entrance offer a lesson from the Buddhas.

433
REAL CANADIAN SUPERSTORE
355 East Kent Avenue North
Aitken Wreglesworth Associates
1988-9

The Superstore burst onto the local scene with its enormous outlets. This one is so big that staff use roller skates. The store and parking lot sit atop a larger distribution centre. The yellow and red suspended metal space frame at the entrance of the structure is repeated in the more elegant gas station (by Nejmark Architects 1990) to the east.

434
SIKH TEMPLE
8000 Ross Street
Erickson/Massey 1969-70

Vancouver's large Sikh population distinguished itself architecturally with its main house of worship. The design, originally unpainted, was inspired by the formal geometry of Indian religious symbols. A simple white block is capped by stepped and diagonally alternating squares crowned by an open steel dome. Ground-floor space occupied by the Khalsa Diwan Society is concealed from the road by landscaping.

435
2000-block Fraserview Drive
1950-1

Central (now Canada) Mortgage and Housing Corporation opened this Fraserview subdivision in 1950 to ease the postwar housing shortage and create a 'workingman's Shaughnessy Heights.' Built mostly by private builders, it consisted of 1,100 houses on curving streets. These small 1½-storey homes with side gables were typical, although many have been altered or replaced.

436
MARIN VISTA
2100-block Waterside & adjacent
Weber & Associate 1984
Riverside and the Fraser Lands (further east) are the names given to an immense swath of former industrial land along the Fraser River, between Argyle Drive and Boundary Road, being redeveloped for residential use. Marin Vista has a marine industrial theme, with gabled units, glazed balconies, and blue 'carpet tile' roofs. Other projects nearby use traditional house forms as sources.

437
FRASER POINTE
3023-43 East Kent Avenue North
Howard/Yano 1990-2
Fraser Pointe, on the Fraser Lands, was built by VLC Properties, the city's arm's-length development wing, to provide rental accommodation to a mix of income levels. It consists of two 14-storey blocks and 8 townhouses. Curved blue balconies protrude from the cream-and-salmon stucco towers. The Phoenix (by Hughes Baldwin 1990-1), just to the east, offers 87 market-priced strata-title suites.

438
LA PETITE MAISON HOUSING
CO-OPERATIVE
Talon Square (off Matheson
Crescent)
Hawthorn/Mansfield/Towers 1978
Champlain Heights was a showcase residential community. The city retained ownership of land, leasing it to developers. Inspired by townhouses around a European square, this stucco and wood co-op has a comfortable, human scale. The first co-op was DeCosmos Village (East 49th at Boundary Road, by Francis Donaldson 1972). Other projects include subsidized rentals and market condos.

Area Twelve **EAST VANCOUVER**

FOUR years before the doors of Gassy Jack's first saloon opened a few miles to the west, Oliver Hocking settled at the north end of the Douglas Road, a trail cut by the Royal Engineers from New Westminster to Burrard Inlet. Hocking soon added a hotel and floating wharf to his holdings and New Brighton, as it came to be called, became British Columbia's first resort. In 1869 a second hotel was added and the name of the young community was changed to Hastings to honour the visit of Admiral George Hastings of the Royal Navy. Throughout the 1870s and 1880s it was a fashionable holiday spot for travellers from the more established centres of New Westminster and even Victoria. Though Hastings can claim to have had the first hotel, post office, and telephone in the area, the opening of the CPR line to its rival Granville effectively ended its pre-eminent position on the south shore of the inlet.

With the prosperity brought by the railway, Vancouver began to slowly expand eastward. The building of the Vancouver–New Westminster interurban railway in 1891 opened up the Grandview area for

settlement, and Vancouver's first suburb soon began to develop along Park (later Commercial) Drive. In the boom period of 1905-12, Grandview filled in rapidly and many substantial homes were built, but the area has always had a working-class feel with most development occurring as comfortable tradesmen's houses on small lots. After the First World War, Grandview began to take on an ethnic flavour, as well, with the arrival of many Italians, East Europeans, and Chinese. After the Second World War, a second wave of Italians arrived bringing to Commercial Drive the lively mix of expresso bars and trattorias it enjoys today.

To the east, the Hastings area was still mainly rural with a number of small farms in the 10- to 20-acre range. In 1889 the provincial government donated 160 acres just south of the Hastings resort as a new park and it soon became known as Hastings Park. The half-mile race track built there drew crowds of Vancouverites who rode the new streetcar line to Grandview and then walked another mile to the races. In 1910 the first, hugely successful, Vancouver Exhibition – renamed the

left: *Vancouver harbour's grain elevators loom like relics of some lost civilization. 'Steven's Folly' is the oldest of these sculptural concrete structures.*

right: *The Quadrangle at Simon Fraser University*

Pacific National Exhibition in 1946 – was held at the park and, also in 1910, the citizens of Hastings voted almost unanimously to end their former association with Burnaby and join Vancouver. The next few decades saw the gradual transformation of Hastings from farmland into a working-class suburb of bungalows on small lots, much like its neighbour Grandview.

The look of East Vancouver has remained remarkably unchanged in recent decades though there has been increasing infiltration of apartment buildings into some residential areas. In the early 1970s, local groups banded together to stop the construction of a freeway down Venables Street, but the area will likely continue to be under pressure to increase the efficiency of transportation between downtown Vancouver and outlying communities.

Simon Fraser University's outstanding architecture cannot be ignored and a summary of the Burnaby Mountain campus is included in this section.

439
BROADWAY SKYTRAIN STATION
Broadway & Commercial
Allen Parker & Associates 1984-5
Rapid transit design usually follows one of two schools. The Montreal Metro exemplifies one – unique stations each designed by a different architect. SkyTrain, in contrast, adopted a uniform look, featuring distinctive tubular steel hoop trusses that wrap around each station and the use of metal mesh instead of glazing. Architektengruppen U-Bahn of Vienna was design consultant on the project.

440
2033-5 East 2nd Avenue
Cotton & Parkin (builders) 1908
Cotton and Parkin were builders and cement contractors who made the 'cast stone' for this duplex on site in a hand-operated block mould – one of the first known uses of concrete blocks in the city. Rusticated quoins provide textural interest, while high side gables and a double front dormer add a picturesque note.

441
VICTORIA COURT
1943 East 1st Avenue
Baynes & Horie 1915
Originally a long-term storage vault for Imperial Bank of Canada records, this attractive brick warehouse, with fine brickwork, cast keystone, and cast relief of the bank's symbol above the cornice, was sensitively converted into townhouses in 1982 (by the Iredale Partnership). New windows and iron balconies are in keeping with the original feeling of the building.

442

ODLUM HOUSE
1774 Grant Street
1905

This residence, for Professor Edward Odlum, was one of the first large houses in Grandview. Odlum was a scientist and theologian of international repute whose many achievements included the development of the first electric light used in Canada. His real love, however, was comparative ethnology, and he travelled extensively to study different cultures, always returning to his Grandview home.

443

HARRIS HOUSE
1210 Lakewood Drive
1908

One of a group of eight virtually identical builders' houses constructed between 1908 and 1910, No. 1210 has been lovingly preserved, both inside and out, by its owners since 1918, the Harris family. Evelyn Harris received a City of Vancouver Heritage Award in 1989 in recognition of her and her family's efforts to maintain the house in its original condition.

444

ST. FRANCIS OF ASSISSI CHURCH & FRIARY
1020 Semlin Street
George Aspell 1938

This little bit of Italy off Commercial Drive, was opened by the Franciscan Order in 1938. The adjacent craftsman house, now a friary for the church, is by Beam and Brown (1909-10) and it features precast concrete balusters on the front entry and fence, and matching wood pillars on the upper balconies.

445
W.H. COPP HOUSE
1110 Victoria Drive
J.P. Malluson 1910-11
Many larger houses, such as this fine Queen Anne mansion for realtor W.H. Copp and the Miller House (446), were built in the Grandview area at the peak of its development around 1910. A domed corner turret, columned portico, and impressive stained and bevelled glass lend elegance to this fine home.

446
KURRAJONG
1036 Salsbury Street
1908
This sprawling Queen Anne mansion was the residence of Alderman John J. Miller, an Australian-born auctioneer, who is credited with almost singlehandedly creating and running the Pacific National Exhibition. Miller Drive in Exhibition Park is named for him. Since the 1930s, the house has operated as the Glen Hospital. Miller named the home after a shrub native to Australia.

447
ROBERTSON PRESBYTERIAN
CHURCH
1795 Napier Street
1908
The vertical strips dividing the walls into 3-foot sections of narrow clapboard are characteristic of the patented BC Mills prefabrication system (see 74). The south wing on Napier Street, now stuccoed (but also a BC Mills prefab), was a later addition (1921). It is now a cultural and education centre for a Fijian religious group.

448
BECK BUILDING
1046 Commercial Drive
c. 1910

One of the original suburbs of the city as it was incorporated in 1896, Grandview developed rapidly following the opening of the Vancouver-New Westminster interurban line in 1891. This elegant, bay-windowed commercial building, with an Italian market on the ground floor and apartments above, is one of many built along Commercial Drive during the construction boom of 1905 to 1912.

449
BRITANNIA COMMUNITY SERVICES CENTRE
1661 Napier Street
Downs/Archambault; Britannia Design 1972-6

A legal partnership between the community, city, and school board led to the creation of this unique centre, fully integrating educational, social, and recreational facilities. Citizen involvement played an important role in the design of this cluster of low, non-institutional looking buildings. Unfortunately, the design does not mesh well with the existing street pattern.

450
VANCOUVER EAST CULTURAL CENTRE
1895 Venables Street
1909

The former Grandview Methodist Church (Grandview United Church after the union of the Methodists and Presbyterians in 1925) reopened in 1973 as a theatre, recital hall, and community facility (alterations and additions by John Keith-King 1973, and Derek Neale 1977). It has since become one of the most popular performing arts venues in the city.

451
STEVENS' FOLLY
North foot of Woodland Drive
1914
Predicting a boom in the international grain trade following the opening of the Panama Canal, Vancouver MP H.H. Stevens induced the Dominion government to build the first grain elevator in Vancouver. Unfortunately, the First World War broke out just as it was completed and it remained idle for the next eight years, the subject of much public ridicule, hence the name 'Stevens' Folly.'

452
GARDEN AUDITORIUM
Exhibition Park
Townley & Matheson 1940
Exhibition Park is home to a fine group of deco and moderne buildings. Of these, the Garden Auditorium is the best. The south façade with its bold, semicircular twin bays is an outstanding piece of moderne styling. Though not of the same high quality, the Forum, Pure Food Building, and the Livestock Building all have good detailing and are worth a look.

453
PACIFIC COLISEUM
Exhibition Park
W.K. Noppe 1966-7
Built to attract a National Hockey League franchise to the city, the original, simple ring of white panels has been much modified since the arena opened in 1967. The Coliseum forms part of the Exhibition Park complex, a 167-acre site that hosts the Pacific National Exhibition each August. Other notable structures in the park include a wooden roller coaster.

454

ALBERTA WHEAT POOL
North foot of Cassiar Street
C.D. Howe Company 1927

The engineering firm founded by C.D. Howe in 1916 was the premier builder of grain elevators. In addition to this one, it designed and built National Harbours Board elevators No. 2 (1955), No. 3 (1936), and No. 4 (1950), the Buckerfields elevator (1927), the Saskatchewan Wheat Pool elevator, and others in Saskatoon, Port Arthur, Toronto, and Buenos Aires.

455

ALBERTA WHEAT POOL OFFICES
North foot of Cassiar Street
Wright Engineers 1991

A surprisingly elegant and sophisticated find in this rough industrial dockland landscape, this high-tech gem is the nerve centre for the largely automated Alberta Wheat Pool complex. Its rounded corners and the vertical lines of its aluminum cladding nicely complement the powerful, almost primeval, power of the elevators themselves.

456

SECOND NARROWS BRIDGE
Highway 401
1960

The present high-level cantilever bridge at Second Narrows is the third at this location. The first was opened in 1925 and the second (both were road and rail bridges) in 1934. A plaque commemorates the eighteen construction workers who were killed in the disastrous collapse of the north anchor arm on 17 June 1958 and the five other workers who died during construction of this third bridge. Note the nearby railway lift bridge (1969).

457
GIRLS' INDUSTRIAL SCHOOL
800 Cassiar Street
A.A. Cox 1912
Opened in 1914 as the Girls' Industrial School, under the administration of the Attorney General's Department, this is one of the best examples of the mission style in the city. It features a formal entrance into an arcaded porch, shaped gables on the dormers, end gables, and moulded window details.

458
SIMON FRASER UNIVERSITY
Burnaby Mountain
Erickson/Massey 1963-5
The first view of this magnificently sited campus atop Burnaby Mountain is truly spectacular. Erickson/Massey's design – the unanimous winner of a competition held by the BC government – was a radical linear scheme that conceived of the new university as a single unit, without the segregation of academic disciplines that characterized traditional campus planning.

459
THE MALL
Simon Fraser University
Erickson/Massey 1963-5
The glass-covered central mall embodies the ideal of the university envisioned in the winning proposal. The scheme shifts the emphasis from individual campus buildings to the pathway between the classroom and the social space of the Mall. The system of glazed metal roof trusses (which failed to keep out the rain) was developed in conjunction with one-time Buckminster Fuller associate, Jeffrey Lindsay.

460
W.A.C. BENNETT LIBRARY
Simon Fraser University
Robert F. Harrison 1963-5
The robust, strongly sculpted form of
the library opens onto the north side of
the Mall. An addition was built in 1976.
The sun louvres mirror those of the Mall
and Academic Quadrangle. The projecting bays hold study carrels. Across the
Mall and opening onto it from the south
are the theatre (by Duncan McNab
1963-5) and the University Centre
Building (by Rhone & Iredale 1973).

461
ACADEMIC QUADRANGLE
Simon Fraser University
Zoltan S. Kiss 1963-5
Massive columns lift the top two floors
of 'the Quad' above a landscaped courtyard. The repetition of sun louvres over
the entire façade echoes the use of vertical elements in the Mall and the library
and gives the entire central campus an
almost classical feel. The courtyard is
tranquil and serene in contrast to the
bustle of the Mall. The Quad's classicism
inspired the comment, by Bruno Freschi,
that SFU would 'make an elegant ruin.'

462
SHRUM SCIENCE COMPLEX
Simon Fraser University
Rhone & Iredale 1963-5
The top five submissions to the competition were awarded prizes and the architects invited to participate in the
creation of the new university. Rhone &
Iredale was the first runner-up and its
contribution is the Shrum Science Complex, which opens off the south side of
the Quadrangle. The science labs are arranged along spiral corridors that lead
from the main concourse down the side
of the ridge.

As evocative a symbol of Vancouver's

railway heritage as the stations themselves

The Royal Hudson, BC Rail Station

Area Thirteen **NORTH VANCOUVER**

A TTRACTED by the magnificent stands of Douglas fir and red cedar that lined the North Shore mountainside, T.W. Graham and George Scrimgeour of New Westminster secured a pre-emption of 150 acres (the first on the north side of Burrard Inlet) in 1862 and opened a sawmill the next year. Their Pioneer Mills soon failed, as did its successor, but in 1865 an entrepreneur from Maine named Sewell Prescott Moody purchased the operation and turned it into an unqualified success. Moody soon held timber rights to over 10,000 acres of North Shore land and kept two mills operating to capacity.

Moodyville outstripped Gastown, its south shore rival, in everything but the number of saloons. It boasted the first school on the inlet (1870) and the first electric lighting system north of San Francisco (1882). It suffered badly, however, during the depression of the 1890s and the mill closed in 1901. No physical evidence remains today of the thriving community of Moodyville, and the site is now occupied by the Saskatchewan Wheat Pool's elevators.

Most of the vast land area from Indian Arm to Howe Sound had

left: *The spacious galleried interior of Lonsdale Quay Market*

right: *The machine shop at Versatile Pacific Shipyards, a typical example of the forceful industrial architecture which gives the currently derelict site its identity and heritage value*

been acquired speculatively by Vancouver interests. In 1891 the landowners were instrumental in incorporating the District of North Vancouver. The depression of the 1890s almost killed the new district, and considerable property was forfeited for unpayed taxes. The Lonsdale Estate and other British interests acquired large holdings in the subsequent tax sales.

When the economy turned upward in the early 1900s, North Vancouver experienced a phenomenal boom. From a population of 365 in 1901, North Vancouver grew to nearly 10,000 by 1907. The exploding settlement became known as the 'Ambitious City.' Fortunes were made in real estate speculation and the city experienced tremendous growth and prosperity. A new commercial area developed at the foot of Lonsdale, a half-mile west of the old Moodyville settlement. By 1911 at least a dozen lumber and shingle mills and several shipyards were in operation. In 1906 the City of North Vancouver separated from the District, and in 1912 the Municipality of West Vancouver, the western half of the District of North Vancouver, was incorporated.

With the disastrous recession of 1913-14 the bubble burst. North Vancouver again suffered badly and, in spite of a boost from wartime shipbuilding, it was not until the late 1920s that growth began again, only to be cut short by the financial crash of 1929. During the depression nearly 75 per cent of all property reverted to the municipalities, who fared little better themselves. The District went into receivership in December 1932 and the city followed a month later. The area found no relief until the Second World War, when its shipyards again benefitted from wartime industries.

The opening of the Lions Gate Bridge in 1938 shifted the focus of the city away from the lower Lonsdale commercial area and the area went into a long, slow decline. Streetcar service was discontinued in 1947 and ferry service stopped in 1958. The revitalization of the area began with the opening of SeaBus service in 1977 and the subsequent Lonsdale Quay development.

463
ST. PAUL'S INDIAN CATHOLIC CHURCH
424 West Esplanade
1909-10

This miniature Gothic cathedral is the centrepiece of an Oblate mission and is more elaborate and faithful to originals in France than most mission churches in BC. It replaced an 1884 building which overlooked tidal flats now filled, and was once a landmark for ships approaching the harbour. Half-paved roads, scattered bungalows, and railway tracks maintain the building's frontier setting.

464
PACIFIC MARINE TRAINING INSTITUTE
265 West Esplanade
Waisman Dewar Grout 1980-1

With its gleaming white metal cladding, integration of circular and rectilinear forms, and ship-like massing, the Pacific Marine Training Institute looks like a BC Ferry dragged onshore. Portholes, metal railings and staircases, and a cluster of flag-flying masts above the 'bridge' all add to the attractive nautical effect.

465
INSURANCE CORPORATION OF BRITISH COLUMBIA
151 West Esplanade
McCarter, Nairne & Partners 1983-4

The huge bulk of this building – the horizontal equivalent of a 23-storey tower – slices through the centre of Lonsdale Quay making for an awkward integration of the eastern and western sections of the site. The building itself with its high-tech external framework, designed to give a column-free interior, achieves a certain industrial monumentality.

466

LONSDALE QUAY MARKET
123 Carrie Cates Court
Hotson Bakker 1985-6

The phenomenal success of Granville Island inspired a host of similar post-industrial revitalization schemes – in New Westminster, for example, and here in North Vancouver. The glazed, galleried market interior pleasingly recalls iron and glass architecture of the 19th century. The market is linked to downtown Vancouver by the SeaBus (a critical factor in the market's success).

467

NORTH VANCOUVER FERRY NO. 5
Foot of Lonsdale Avenue
West Coast Salvage & Contracting Company 1941

The only survivor from a fleet of harbour ferries, this ship was taken out of service in 1958 but rebuilt as the Seven Seas restaurant. The new owner added the neon sign, now something of a period piece itself. Wood panelling, engines, and nautical ambience have been retained. The vessel is moored near its original ferry slip.

468

VERSATILE PACIFIC SHIPYARD
206-67 West Esplanade

Some of the best industrial architecture in the city can be found at this historically important site, currently derelict but with the potential for creative reuse. Originally Wallace Shipyards, and later Burrard Dry Dock, the yard was founded in 1894 on False Creek and moved to the North Shore in 1906. It was once the mainstay of North Vancouver's economy – 10,000 people worked here during the Second World War.

469

BANK OF HAMILTON CHAMBERS
92 Lonsdale Avenue
Mills & Hutton 1910-11

Stoutly set on a sloping corner, this former bank is distinguished by fine Greco-Roman detail on the façade and cornice, cast-iron lights, and the original elevator inside (the first to be installed on the North Shore). The Bank of Hamilton and the adjacent Aberdeen Block (470), forming a pleasing Edwardian streetscape, are relics of a brief building boom which never quite made it up the hill.

470

ABERDEEN BLOCK
90 Lonsdale Avenue
Mills & Hutton 1910-11

This elegant exercise in Edwardian commercial design has been home to Paine Hardware since 1912. The BC Electric Railway Company, which operated North Vancouver's streetcars, had its offices here. While under construction, the building was known as the Keith Block, hence the letter 'K' in the stone shield above the entry.

471

BC TELEPHONE COMPANY
117 West 1st Street
BC Telephone Building
Department 1926

This four-square little gem, originally the commercial offices of the BC Telephone Company and now a photographer's studio, features a finely detailed pediment and brickwork relieved with concrete trim. The original tilework, granite front step, copper sashed windows, and even the small flag brackets on the storefront are intact and well preserved.

472
THE OBSERVATORY
120 West 2nd Street
Hulbert Group 1989

This condominium building offers residents spectacular views of the mountains and Burrard Inlet – more than can be said for its appearance from the street. Private versus public views, and 'view corridors' continue to provoke debate in Vancouver. The tallest building on the North Shore, the Observatory was built just before a height restriction was imposed on historic Lower Lonsdale.

473
JONES HOUSE
408 East 2nd Street
1906

A variation on the BC Mills prefabrication system, here with an added second storey, this home for BC Electric Railway conductor W.D. Jones has been rehabilitated, and a sensitive infill building, which takes up the batten and panel motif of the original house, added to the west and north (by Cornerstone Architects 1991-2).

474
214 West 6th Street
1907

Wide, flat eaves and a campanile-like 3-storey tower bring a touch of Tuscany to this exceptional villa thought to have been a showhome for the North Vancouver Land and Improvement Company's Ottawa Gardens development. The porch is a later addition, not unsympathetic to the original Italianate design.

475
STEPHENS HOUSE
234 West 6th Street
Mackay & Mackay 1911

Ottawa Gardens was planned, like the later Grand Boulevard, as an exclusive residential district. Much of its character is still evident with several fine old homes overlooking the landscaped boulevard. Precast concrete blocks imitate stone on this house owned by Thomas Stephens who worked for Leckie Shoes in Gastown (14).

476
LARSON HOUSE
254 West 6th Street
Blackadder & Mackay 1921

This is a very good example of the craftsman style, asymmetrically composed with an offset gabled entrance, porch brackets, half-timbering, and a wide-eaved dormer window. The date of construction is significant as development of Ottawa Gardens and Grand Boulevard was interrupted by the First World War.

477
FIRST CHURCH OF CHRIST, SCIENTIST
185 Keith Road East
Honeyman & Curtis 1925

Small but elegantly proportioned and beautifully sited at the east end of Victoria Park, this church features a semicircular porch, corner pilasters, and exceptional detailing on the entry and windows. Christian Science has always preferred classically inspired forms and prominent beaux-arts inspired sites.

478
ST. ANDREWS UNITED CHURCH
1044 St. Georges Avenue
Alexander & Brown 1912

Presbyterian before the union with the Methodists in 1925 created the United Church, St. Andrews is a vigorous exercise in the Gothic revival style. Located at the top of a hill where the streets change their orientation, its tall spire makes it a prominent local landmark.

479
225, 227, 229 East 10th Street
Gladwin Benson (builder) 1910

Like three bottles of vintage wine standing out from the cases of suburban plonk which line most North Vancouver streetscapes, these three identical Edwardian homes are all well preserved in their original verandahed formality. A comparable group can be seen at Barclay Square Heritage Park in the West End.

480
RIDGEWAY SCHOOL
420 East 8th Street
Jones & Gillam 1911-12

This is an enjoyable mélange of florid Edwardian baroque accented with Georgian revival brickwork, Bavarian schloss doorways, and a châteauesque roofline topped by an arts and crafts cupola. The wings, later added (by Benzie & Bow 1926), decline to compete with the original centrepiece. Note the more conservative, Palladian style Queen Mary School (1915) at 230 Keith Road.

481
GILL HOUSE
1617 Grand Boulevard
N.A. Kearns 1911-12

Touted as the finest residential avenue in Canada when it was conceived in 1906 by the North Vancouver Land & Improvement Company, Grand Boulevard has never quite lived up to its name. Many larger homes, like this unusual design for one-time councillor and reeve of the District of North Vancouver, James C. Gill, were completed but the collapse of the 1905-12 construction boom put an end to such grand pretensions.

482
LIONS GATE HOSPITAL
230 East 13th Street
Benzie & Bow 1929

William Bow, who later went on to work on the Lions Gate Bridge (235), was instructed by the hospital board to provide 'little in the manner of frills' for their new hospital. Given these constraints, Bow produced a surprising châteauesque/art deco design in brick, concrete, and stucco. Third-storey additions were added to the two wings in 1948.

483
ST. JOHN THE EVANGELIST
ANGLICAN CHURCH
220 West 8th Street
Keith Watson-Donald 1987

This postmodern design shows some Scottish influence in the crow-stepped gable on 8th Street. The interior space is confident and serene, but the exterior focus seems diffuse. Note North Vancouver Civic Centre (Downs/Archambault 1974), 121 West 14th Street, which also attempts to formalize a difficult site.

484

VANCE HOUSE
620 West 15th Street
1910

An exceptional Edwardian house, this was the home of George Washington Vance, long-time alderman and mayor of North Vancouver (from 1917 to 1921). The house has been restored and sensitively integrated within a new housing complex (by Noort Developments 1990) beautifully sited around a courtyard overlooking a densely forested ravine.

485

BC RAIL STATION
1311 West 1st Street
Hale & Harrison 1956

The southern terminus of BC Rail – formerly the Pacific Great Eastern Railway – this station looked futuristic in its day, but alterations have marred its clean lines and glazed surfaces. During the summer, the Royal Hudson steam train takes tourists from here up Howe Sound to Squamish. Year-round diesel service continues northward along the scenic line to Lillooet and Prince George.

486

1300-block Whitewood Crescent
1949-51

This is one of the least altered blocks in the Norgate neighbourhood and an example of idealistic postwar planning. The ranch-style bungalows, each prefabricated and assembled on a concrete slab, used underfloor 'radiant heat' and other progressive ideas. A linear park runs east-west from the community school at Redwood Street to Tatlow Avenue.

487
3749 Edgemont Boulevard
Fred Hollingsworth 1950-1

One of several fourplex units designed in the energetic modernism espoused by local architects during the postwar years, this block shows the influence through horizontal massing and over-hung eaves of the Frank Lloyd Wright prairie style. The architect's own house (1948) can be glimpsed nearby at 1205 Ridgewood Drive.

488
CAPILANO SUSPENSION BRIDGE
3735 Capilano Road

Scottish engineer George Grant Mackay moved to BC after being tempted by the Canadian display at the Glasgow International Exhibition of 1888. He developed land around the Capilano gorge, envisioning a 'recreational area for the benefit of all,' and built the first bridge in 1889. The current bridge (1903, rebuilt 1914 and 1956) shares the site with an eccentric group of cabins and totem poles.

489
CAPILANO FISH HATCHERY
4500 Capilano Road
Underwood, McKinley & Wilson 1979-80

This concrete and wood building, nestled in the Capilano River gorge, flows across the rocky riverbank with the same ease as the salmon swimming in the display tanks inside the building. Well-planned indoor/outdoor circulation in the public areas allows study of the exhibits and the river as one.

490
CLEVELAND DAM
Capilano Regional Park
J. T. Savage (engineer) 1954
Lake Capilano, a source of Vancouver's drinking water, was created behind this 300-foot-high concrete dam whose rugged engineering is as dramatic as the gorge it spans. The dam was named after E.A. Cleveland, the first chief commissioner of the Greater Vancouver Water District. Cleveland was also one of the party who named Grouse Mountain after the blue grouse they shot on it in 1894.

491
GROUSE MOUNTAIN CHALET
6400 Nancy Green Way
Peter Kaffka 1956
This angular, almost expressionist, cedar chalet is reached by a precipitous cable-car ascent offering panoramic views of Vancouver, almost 4,000 feet below. In the 1920s you could drive up the mountain to a sprawling, rustic chalet, since demolished. McCarter & Nairne proposed a sweeping, moderne replacement in 1938 which was never built.

492
4342 Skyline Drive
1954
An expressive roofline continuing over the car port and front door enlivens this California-influenced timber-frame house. The large geometrically framed window forming the front gable is typical of this particular and much imitated form of vernacular modernism. Note the Ron Thom house further down the hill at 3600 Glenview Drive (c. 1955), constructed inside and out of plywood sheeting.

493
3490 Fairmont Road
Arthur J. Mudry 1985

This convincing and respectful Frank Lloyd Wright-influenced design, a conversion of a 1955 single-storey home, recalls the early prairie style first developed in the suburbs of Chicago before the First World War. The horizontal emphasis, wide overhanging eaves, and low-slung hipped roof are conventional features of the style here revived with the novelty of a Richardsonian-inspired arched entrance.

494
300-block Cartelier Place
Hassell Griblin Associates
c. 1972

An example of West Coast regionalism at its best, this excellent group of woodsy tree houses, designed with seemingly casual abandon, conceals a sophisticated response to the steeply irregular, wooded topography. Cedar construction and split-level interior skylit spaces create an effect of whispered intimacy which only the houses and the forest share. Note the Japanese-style home at 329 Cartelier Road.

495
RONALD HOUSE
134 Queens Road West
1913

This attractive craftsman or 'California bungalow' home is an early example of a style that would sweep Vancouver in the decade following the First World War. It features some good stained and leaded glass, and wide projecting eaves suggestive of Frank Lloyd Wright and the prairie school. The house next door (No. 144), built the year before, is more typical of the prewar decade.

496
NYE HOUSE
230 Carisbrooke Road East
Henry Blackadder 1912
Boer War veteran Thomas Nye made a fortune in land speculation and, it is said, lost it building this imposing North Lonsdale Tudor revival home. The house was extensively damaged by fire in 1990 and has undergone restoration. Two in-fill houses (by Dick Goldhammer 1989) mirror the design of the Nye house.

497
FROMME HOUSE
1466 Ross Road
1900
Lumberman Julius M. Fromme home-steaded here in 1899 and built this sim-ple house – the first built in the Lynn Valley area – facing the skid road (whence its angled orientation to the street). Fromme's Lynn Valley Lumber Company logged the west bank of Lynn Creek and processed the logs a few blocks away in his mill at Lynn Valley Road and Mountain Highway.

498
ST. PIUS X CHURCH
1150 Indian River Drive
Downs/Archambault 1980
This surprising church, a fascinating postmodern essay in Tuscan revivalism, follows Romanesque precepts with a simple interior, illuminated with natural light from its clerestory windows, en-tered from an arched doorway. Pleas-antly planned in a forested setting, the brick church and stuccoed rectory and church office building are grouped around an open-sided courtyard.

Leaping dramatically from

Stanley Park's Prospect Point

Lions Gate Bridge

Area Fourteen **WEST VANCOUVER**

I N the 1870s, the old growth forest west of the Capilano River on the North Shore was logged and exported via Hastings Mill and Moodyville (North Vancouver) to Europe, Asia, and Australia. Land was claimed by logging companies and investors, but transportation was difficult, except by water, and only a few sparsely populated settlements developed, such as Caulfeild village and at the Point Atkinson lighthouse.

Attempts to link the area with North Vancouver, along what is now Keith Road, were never completed. But in 1909 realtor John Lawson began a scheduled ferry service to Vancouver from Ambleside which prompted a flurry of speculation and development. Three years later, the Municipality of West Vancouver was incorporated. It encompassed the territory from the Capilano River to Howe Sound. Despite the rough terrain, roads were laid out in grid pattern as they had been in North Vancouver. Only west of 26th Street in West Vancouver, and on the higher elevations of both districts, does the street plan nestle into the topography.

West Vancouver failed to attract industry, although the Pacific Great Eastern Railway (now BC Rail) had built a line from North Vancouver to Whytecliff (near Horseshoe Bay) in 1914. The line operated as a commuter route for a while but then lay dormant until it was connected to the interior in 1956. Homeowners who had bought property on the route were unpleasantly surprised when the railway right-of-way was reactivated.

In 1925 West Vancouver's city fathers decided to make their community exclusively residential. The following year they adopted a Town Planning Act that banned industry and set standards for building lot sizes. These restrictions attracted the Irish Guinness family and a group of British investors who formed British Pacific Properties Limited. During the depression they bought a major portion of the municipality (and the Marine Building in Vancouver) and proceeded with residential development. Later in the 1930s, the same group linked their land to Vancouver by the Lions Gate Bridge, assuring West Vancouver's status as a prosperous dormitory suburb. Since the war, shopping and com-

left: *From a distance, parts of West Vancouver appear like hill towns in Tuscany, but close up, the district's topography is being bulldozed by relentless suburban development.*

right: *The Smith House, an example of how the West Coast style sensitively blends architecture with the landscape into which it intrudes*

mercial facilities have developed at Park Royal, Ambleside, Dunderave, Upper Caulfeild, and Horseshoe Bay, the latter a busy ferry terminal since the completion of the Upper Levels Highway in the 1970s.

West Vancouver, with its prosperity and rugged natural setting, has been a fertile ground for residential architects. The West Coast style (variously derived from Frank Lloyd Wright, the Greene brothers, and Bernard Maybeck in early twentieth-century California, European modernism, and Japanese tradition) is strongly represented. But the fine example set by B.C. Binning, Ron Thom, and Arthur Erickson, and others, whose work responds with sensitivity and respect for the natural surroundings, unfortunately seems lost on some contemporary developers, whose arid suburbia is relentlessly climbing the slopes to the 1,200-foot elevation limit of permitted development.

499
PARK ROYAL SHOPPING CENTRE
Marine Drive & Taylor Way
C.B.K. Van Norman; J.C. Page 1950
Built with Guinness money partly on land acquired from the Capilano Indian Band, this is one of the first two shopping centres in Canada. The much altered original complex is on the north side of Marine Drive. Park Royal south (by John Graham Jr.) was added in 1962. The aging complex received an early 1990s facelift in predictable postmodern style.

500
CAPILANO GOLF & COUNTRY CLUB
420 Southborough Drive
Olmsted Brothers (landscape architects)
Developed as part of British Pacific Properties, this is one of the most scenic links in the country. The landscaping and Scottish Highland/mock-Tudor clubhouse is by J.F. Dawson of Olmsted Brothers, Massachussetts (successors to Frederick Law Olmsted, designer of Mount Royal Park, Montreal, and Central Park, New York). The Olmsted firm also planned the layout of the properties.

501
EPPICH HOUSE
1056 Groveland Road
Arthur Erickson 1983
Glass blocks and curving steel cascade from the hillside to compose this three-level home with taut energy rather than repose. The owner's industries facilitated the steel fabrication of this home, completed over 10 years. Contrast with the earlier Eppich House (1972) at 1812 Palmerston Avenue, designed in the architect's more familiar concrete and wood, post-and-beam style. Both gardens employ creative watery effects.

502
855 King George Way
Ernest Collins 1992

'Monster houses' proliferate in the British Properties, adding to the pot-pourri of styles in the area but ignoring the 'garden city' ethos by which the neighbourhood was originally planned. Few match this grotesque Georgian revival composition which pretentiously attempts to play the correct tune but manages, through overemphasis, to strike all the wrong notes in an enjoyably kitsch performance.

503
WU HOUSE
1247 Chartwell Place
Erickson/Massey 1967

Designed like many homes in West Vancouver for privacy and views, this strongly geometric design by Bruno Freschi turns away from the street to overlook a gully and stream. Terraced levels at the rear are unified by the steep slope of the roof. Inventive sculptural chimneys surmount a baffle of thin wooden slats which act as a deflective rain screen on the roof and walls.

504
SPENCER HOUSE
2089 Westdean Crescent
1913

This large craftsman bungalow was owned by Thomas Arthur Spencer, son of department store owner David Spencer. The house originally over-looked the Spencer estate, which sloped down to Mathers Avenue. The estate has long been subdivided, but the house retains many period features, including half-timbering, river-stone trim, and an expansive verandah extending to a porte-cochère.

505
PORTER HOUSE
1560 Ottawa Avenue
J.C.H. Porter 1948-9

An influential example of Vancouver post-and-beam modernism, this house was a Massey Medal winner, rated 'best house in Canada.' The innovative structure of this house, and those of Porter's contemporaries, Ned Pratt, Duncan Mc-Nab, Peter Thornton, and Roy Jessiman, captivated the housing market of the day. Mass-produced versions, notably by Lewis Construction, were built (and can still be found) on the North Shore.

506
885 Braeside Avenue
Ross A. Lort 1942

This delightful olde English cottage is of a type more often seen on Christmas cards and cake tins. Half-timbering, leaded glass, textured brick and stone, and heat-formed shingles imitating a thatched roof are employed to picturesque effect, and are repeated by the same builder (see 379) at two other locations.

507
AMBLESIDE PARK 'GRANITE ASSEMBLAGE'
Foot of 14th Street
Don Vaughan 1989

This imaginative water sculpture, commissioned as part of the Ambleside revitalization project, is animated by the interplay of granite blocks, fluidity, and texture (a response to the vitality of the harbour and tidal shoreline), and enobled by its classical reference suggestive of the collapsed columns of ancient Greece and Rome.

508
FERRY BUILDING
Foot of 14th Street
Thompson & Campbell 1913

Designed in rural railway station style, this was formerly the ticket office and waiting room for the ferries which once sailed over to downtown Vancouver. It was restored in 1988 by Howard/Yano Architects as an art gallery, forming, with the rebuilt pier and a water sculpture (507), a pleasant waterfront ensemble.

509
'NAVVY JACK' THOMAS HOUSE
1768 Argyle Avenue
c. 1873

Although much altered, this is still considered one of the oldest homes on the lower mainland. Welshman John Thomas joined the Cariboo gold rush of 1858, later ran a ferry service on Burrard Inlet, and invested in waterfront property, before falling on hard times and losing the house in 1892.

510
WEST VANCOUVER MUNICIPAL HALL
750 17th Street
Toby, Russell & Buckwell 1964

Built on the site of the original municipal hall (the land was purchased from John Lawson for one dollar), this 3-storey building features a strong trapezoidal motif which is reflected in the sloped undersides of the projecting concrete slabs, the incised precast panels on the ground floor, the etching on the windows, and on the door handles. Firehall No. 1, across 16th Street, is by the same architects (1967).

511
LAWSON HOUSE
680 17th Street
1940

With the first mortgage ever granted to a woman in British Columbia, Gertrude Lawson built this solid, eclectic 'period' house. The stone was carried as ships' ballast from New Zealand and saved by her father, John Lawson. One of Greater Vancouver's few stone houses, it has been converted (Toby, Russell, Buckwell & Partners 1992) for museum use.

512
WAR MEMORIAL
Memorial Park
1925

This undemonstrative war memorial is all the more effective for the absence of the strident poignancy usually found on such monuments. The rough stone gateway, which acts as an entrance to Memorial Park, is suggestive of plans never completed and is quietly moving in its apparently abandoned state.

513
CRESCENT APARTMENTS
2135 Argyle Street
Warnett Kennedy & Kenneth
Gardner 1961

The first high rise in West Vancouver, this building was designed to offer both privacy and panoramic views from its sweeping, curved balconies. The latter, are curiously low-tech, with parapets formed with split terracotta water pipes to save weight and add decoration. Note the rear elevation with its boldly glazed stairway.

514

LES TERRACES
2250 Bellevue Avenue
Matsuzaki, Wright
1990-1

This excellent building radiates poise, authority, structural honesty, and stylish restraint. Postmodern frippery is ignored for constructivist vigour which is especially evident in the use of visible, stepbacked columns and beams handled in Erickson fashion and reminiscent of the Provincial Law Courts at Robson Square (136).

515

MORSE HOUSE
2843 Marine Drive
Lewis Morse (designer) 1989

A crisp composition of triangles and squares held together by the consistent use of shingles throughout (even on the fence), this broadly Cape Cod style creekside residence presents a closed aspect to the street but opens out on the garden side. It forms a pair with its next-door neighbour to the east, also by Lewis Morse.

516

WEST VANCOUVER
PRESBYTERIAN CHURCH
2893 Marine Drive
Hamish McIntyre 1965

This romantic A-frame design, suggestive of mysterious forces and haunted forests, seems medieval and Nordic in inspiration. Projecting, angled timbers punched through the roof apex emphasize the church's reference to its wooded milieu and help the design overcome a disappointing entrance. The interior is as impressively moody as the roof implies.

517
BENNETT HOUSE
2909 Mathers Avenue
1937

Curved stucco walls, corner windows, and glass block detailing all identify this as an essay in the moderne style, popular for factory and office buildings in the 1930s, but less frequently seen in domestic architecture. Above it, at 1660 29th Street, is another handsome, but altered, moderne home, the Langley House (1938), designed by H.C. Berchten-Breiter.

518
B.C. BINNING HOUSE
2968 Mathers Crescent
B.C. Binning; Sharp & Thompson,
Berwick, Pratt (consulting
architects) 1941

This trend-setting example of modernism in Vancouver was designed and decorated by artist and teacher B.C. Binning, local champion of modern art and architecture in a city with a penchant for mock-Tudor. The international style's flat roof, modular arrangement of the interior space, and glazed southern exposure were a radical change from the cozy conventions of the time.

519
221 Maple Lane
1982

Radcliffe Avenue and Maple Lane, narrow winding roads along a rocky ledge above the sea, typify the charm of West Vancouver. An eclectic mix of housing ranges from craftsman, such as the Hewitt House at 3321 Radcliffe (1923), to this elegant expression of the West Coast style on Maple Lane, reached via a bridge across a small creek.

520
130 South Oxley
Fred Hollingsworth 1992-3
Architect Hollinsworth's earlier prairie style (see 486) explodes in this breathtaking postmodern house – or is it a beached Jules Verne submarine? The wonderfully eccentric composition, with sweeping, layered horizontals, curvaceous corners, and Gaudiesque chimneys, while owing a debt to late Wright, also seems inspired, in true organic fashion, by large seashells found on the shore.

521
SNODDY HOUSE
3666 Marine Drive
1929
Spectacularly sited between Marine Drive and the sea, this home for Captain Summersgill Snoddy, a pilot for the BC Pilotage Authority, was originally a small beachside house. Rebuilt in 1939, its strong vertical lines and stark whiteness were a daring contrast to the craftsman- and Tudor revival-derived styles with their horizontal massing and emphasis on natural materials.

522
GREENE HOUSE
4646 Clovelly Walk
Patkau Architects 1991
Sophisticated in its use of form and meticulously crafted, this modern house is enriched by a timber-braced, barrel-vaulted livingroom, seamlessly integrated into the open plan interior but expressed as a single formal space. A secluded entrance courtyard, slightly Mediterranean, creates a sense of tradition and occasion, contrasting with the home's quirky style and precipitous location.

523
ST. FRANCIS IN THE WOOD
4773 Piccadilly South
H.A. Stone 1927

This charming English village church is named after St. Francis of Assisi who is remembered inside in stained glass made by Morris and Company, London. William Morris's rustic socialism was the inspiration for Caulfeild village, planned, with arts and crafts sensibility, by Francis Caulfeild who had arrived from England in 1888 and settled at Caulfeild Cove the following year.

524
WEST VANCOUVER FIRE HALL NO. 3
4895 Marine Drive
Eng & Wright 1982

A functional low-tech building reworks traditional fire station typology (see 253 & 419) in a refreshingly honest manner. Corrugated sheeting and brickwork on a concrete frame are vividly coloured bringing an almost childish (in the best sense) faith and a certain reassurance of old-fashioned reliability to the design and its purpose.

525
4239 Rockridge Crescent
John Kay 1986

This striking, almost fortress-like, home, pays homage to Frank Lloyd Wright. Horizontal decks, overhangs, and step-backed concrete landscaping contrive an organic effect implying that the building – its wooden siding painted grey to match the rocky outcrops behind – has been carved from, rather than built on, the site.

526
POINT ATKINSON LIGHT-HOUSE
Lighthouse Park
Colonel William Anderson 1911-12

One of the few remaining manned lights on the West Coast, the lighthouse is beautifully set amidst a group of white clapboard ancillary buildings. The first light (1874) was replaced by this hexagonal buttressed concrete beacon – an offspring of Anderson's finest creation, a 150-foot-high concrete tower, braced by flying buttresses and built in 1909 at Estevan Point, Vancouver Island.

527
SMITH HOUSE
5030 The Byway
Erickson/Massey 1965

The poetic suffusion of house into landscape and vice versa – the essence of the West Coast style – is here handled with urbane rather than rustic sensibility. Japanese influence shows in the home's austerity and structural poise (although the posts and beams are muscular like Native timber houses) and in the reflecting pool in the small central courtyard. Note the studio addition (by Russell Hollingsworth 1990).

528
KEW HOUSE
Kew Beach
Palmer & Bow 1937

Built on an estate named after Kew Gardens in London, this Spanish colonial/provincial French house belonged to A.J.T. Taylor, president of British Pacific Properties, whose extensive land holdings were (and still are) being developed. Taylor and his family lived in the penthouse of the Marine Building (171) until this house was built.

529
MONTEVERDI ESTATES
5354 Marine Drive
Arthur Erickson 1979

This is an elegant example of the kind of housing that can be developed on West Vancouver's steep forested hillsides in contrast to the faceless 'McMansions' that are beginning to sprawl over ridge and bowl above the Upper Levels Highway. Twenty homes, based on a prototype unit, which can be varied in size and internal articulation, are artfully arranged on the 7-acre site.

530
HASSELL HOUSE
5791 Telegraph Trail
Robert Hassell 1966

Robert Hassell designed his compact home while still a student at UBC's School of Architecture. The house, with its vertical siding (of cheap reject cedar) and shed roof has been emulated throughout the Vancouver area. Hassell and partner Barry Griblin also designed the nearby J.C. Weill house at 5873 Marine Drive (1972-3). Note 5762 Larson Place, a neo-Gothic tree house by Paul Merrick.

531
RUSSELL HOLLINGSWORTH HOUSE
5747 Marine Drive
Russell Hollingsworth 1977-82

Finished with the delicacy of a Japanese lacquered box, this refined West Coast style home successfully fuses traditional oriental and European modernist sources with touches of California. Concrete, petrified like lava, fills the cavities of the rocky site to provide a smooth surface on which the house is composed and displayed.

532
GLENEAGLES CLUBHOUSE
6155 Gleneagles Drive
1928

This building, with its attractive Bavarian-cum-mock-Tudor design, was formerly the club house of the Gleneagles Golf and Country Club. Paired with a later companion, the clubhouse is outwardly quite well preserved, having been converted into a private home. Gleneagles Drive leads to one of the area's secluded coves. Many West Vancouver homes are, in fact, best seen from the waterfront.

533
BARRY DOWNS HOUSE
6664 Marine Drive
Barry Downs 1979

This precarious split-level home clinging to the cliffside takes the West Coast style's marriage to nature to a precipitous extreme. Intimate interior spaces, designed to a diminutive scale but cleverly luminous, step up and down in echoing response to the clifftop's ridges and hollows. The simple barn-like carport and bridge to the house are attractive idiosyncrasies.

534
6991 Hycroft Road
Thompson, Berwick & Pratt 1961

Expressive use of form, with a long single storey abruptly rising to a wide-eaved upper floor turned 90 degrees to frame a sundeck not seen from the street, distinguishes this Ron Thom design, which makes the most of a wonderful location around the point from Horseshoe Bay and overlooking Howe Sound. One of Thom's most influential West Coast designs, the D.H. Copp house, is illustrated on page 258.

Parapet detailing and a minaret bring an exotic flavour to this design.

St. James Anglican Church

Guide to Architectural Styles

Note: Numbers after names of buildings indicate that there is a corresponding entry in the text.

ART DECO
Marine Building (171)
The name 'art deco' was derived from an exhibition on art and the machine age, the 'Exposition Internationale des Arts Décoratifs et Industriels Moderne,' held in Paris in 1925. The style, popular from the late 1920s to the Second World War, rejected traditional ornament and substituted decoration based on geometric patterns of transport and industry mixed with styles of ornament from Mayan and Egyptian sources. Lavish materials and rich colours were combined to produce conspicuously theatrical effects.

ARTS AND CRAFTS
Canterbury House (406)
The English arts and crafts movement of the late 19th century (the source of this style) emphasized craftsmanship, local materials, and strived for a picturesque effect. Arts and crafts buildings are normally asymmetrical with prominent steeply pitched roofs, a varied gable sequence, and eaves overhangs. Surface treatment includes rough-cast stucco and shingles with brick or stone used for chimneys and foundations.

BEAUX-ARTS CLASSICISM
Dominion Building (110)
Named after the Ecole des Beaux-Arts, the state architecture school in Paris and the premier school of its type in the late 19th century, this style is frequently seen in major institutional and commercial buildings. It displays a luxuriant and decorative interpretation of classical motifs based on principles of formal planning. The style features decorative and deeply shadowed sculptural effects, vigorously paired columns, and round-headed or broken pediments.

BOOMTOWN
400-block Powell Street
Common in Vancouver's pre-fire and immediate post-fire commercial architecture, these buildings have a gabled roof hidden behind a false front, which is intended to lend an air of substance to an otherwise plain wood-frame pioneer structure. A cornice was often added to bolster the sense of dignity and permanence. Original examples are rare. Many have been stuccoed or otherwise altered.

BRUTALISM
W.A.C. Bennett Library (460)
Brutalism is predominantly a style of concrete. Brutalist buildings have massive walls, often left in roughly patterned concrete. Arthur Erickson's comment (referring to Simon Fraser University), 'Here unfinished concrete ... becomes as noble a material as any limestone,' expresses the aesthetic well. The term 'brutalism' comes from the French expression *béton brut*, meaning rough concrete.

CHATEAU STYLE

Hotel Vancouver (181)
Based on the castles of the Loire Valley, the style was popular for landmark commercial or institutional buildings. In Canada, every major city boasts its château style hotel built by one of the nation's railways. A steeply pitched copper roof, dormers, windows, and pseudo-Renaissance ornament are the main identifying characteristics. Scottish baronial, Gothic, and classical details are frequently blended in an elaborate mélange which was once promoted as *the* Canadian architectural style.

CRAFTSMAN

2900-block West 5th Avenue (352)
The craftsman bungalow dominated Vancouver domestic building after 1910. The name 'bungalow' comes from India; the Vancouver version of the style originated in California (hence it is the 'California bungalow'). Craftsman bungalows have low-pitched gabled roofs with broad overhangs, exposed rafters and beams, eaves brackets, and wood siding or shingles. Porch supports are usually stubby with sides sloping to the base. The style was also popular for large houses.

EDWARDIAN BUILDER

800-block Broughton Street
These houses are 2 or 2½ stories with a hipped roof. Earlier versions (c. 1905-10) are undecorated; later examples may have bay windows and ornamentation. Porches are common and some classical detailing (columns and decorative mouldings) may also be found. Surface treatment is usually narrow lapped wooden siding but some homes were built with precast concrete blocks. The style is also known as 'foursquare.'

253

EDWARDIAN COMMERCIAL
Manhattan Apartments (178)
These buildings are boldly composed in classical fashion with regular fenestration, flat roofs, and cornices. They may be four to twelve storeys high with brick or stone walls over a steel, concrete, or heavy-timber structural frame with façades treated as three distinct parts: an ornamented ground floor; the plainer main portion, with windows often set in brick or terracotta; and top floors frequently ornamented and with a heavily bracketed cornice.

GEORGIAN REVIVAL
5326 Connaught Drive (337)
Georgian revival buildings, inspired by the architecture of 18th-century Britain, are generally rectangular in plan and symmetrical in form. They are usually two or three storeys high and three to five bays wide, with a central entrance often with a pedimented door or columned portico. Ornamentation is derived from classical styles. Shutters are common in the American 'federal' or 'colonial' variant. Walls may be brick with stone quoins or wood clapboard with quoins or corner strips.

GOTHIC REVIVAL
St. Paul's Indian Catholic Church (463)
The Gothic revival was introduced into Canada in the early years of the 19th century and became the preferred style for both Protestant and Catholic church architecture. The style is characterized by pointed-arch windows (often with hood mouldings), steeply pitched roofs, gables with fretwork or other ornament, and buttresses. Many Vancouver Gothic revival churches have stone walls. Shingled walls are found on less elaborate examples.

HIGH-TECH

Insurance Corporation of British Columbia (465)

This futuristic style of building empha-sizes precision and technology with pipes for air conditioning and water of-ten exposed and brightly coloured. Structural elements are prominently dis-played, especially where they are innova-tive or unusual. Off-the-shelf industrial materials, stainless steel, and aluminum are frequently employed, although the true high-tech building is specially made and assembled for a specific site.

INTERNATIONAL STYLE

Vancouver Public Library (180)

Derived from the Bauhaus-inspired, avant-garde European style of the 1920s, the international style is characterized by flat roofs, smooth and uniform wall sur-faces, often highly glazed, and a com-plete denial of historical ornament. Most of the major commercial and institu-tional buildings from the 1950s to the 1970s in Vancouver are of this style. Steel, glass, and polished stone are the dominant materials, often assembled with precise, elegant geometry.

ITALIANATE

Masonic Temple (25)

This style, common among commercial buildings in the 1880s, is characterized by rows of arched windows. A combina-tion of round, segmental, and stilted-seg-mental arches are common, usually varied on each floor. Mouldings fre-quently feature colours, materials, or textures which give the façades pic-turesque quality. Cornices are often bracketed, and the ground floor may be a shop front with large flat-headed win-dows and cast-iron mullions.

MODERNE
American Can Company (72)

Closely related to art deco, moderne buildings are geometric in composition and often 'streamlined' with sweeping curved corners. Wall spaces are smoothly finished stucco, stone, or concrete, either plain or set off with fluted pilasters, panels, or low-relief art deco ornament. Glass blocks are often used in domestic examples. The style was considered fashionable and futuristic when it was introduced in the late 1920s and it continued in Vancouver until around 1950.

NEOCLASSICAL REVIVAL
Canadian Imperial Bank of Commerce (154)

Neoclassical buildings are characterized by classical motifs composed with an uncluttered, rigorous effect, quieter than beaux-arts classicism. Pediments and porticos project from the façades in a grand manner. Decoration is reduced to a minimum and the columns, entablatures, arches, and any decorative carving adhere to Greek or Roman temple precedents, which were considered the highest expression of classical form.

PIONEER
1000-block Richards Street

These early and modest houses are usually 1¹/₂ (but sometimes 2 or 2¹/₂) storeys high with a gabled roof facing the street, the entrance under the gable, and perhaps a simple porch or verandah. They are usually faced with shiplap or narrow clapboard siding (the latter becoming prevalent around 1900). A shed-roofed kitchen is common at the rear. Most pioneer houses pre-date the building boom of 1907-12.

POSTMODERN
1100-block Robson Street
Postmodernism (or Po Mo) in architecture is a reaction to the perceived sterility, monotony, and austerity of the international style. Po Mo architects reintroduce historical allusion, ornament, and colourful materials to enliven their work. At its best, this style can be lively, surprising, picturesque, and even amusing, but it frequently declines into vulgarity and meaningless historicism.

QUEEN ANNE
1612 Cedar Crescent
Queen Anne buildings (most of them houses) are picturesque and asymmetrical in composition. They feature steeply pitched roofs and numerous projecting features, such as bay and dormer windows, turrets, and wide verandas. Extensive ornamentation is used throughout. Shingles, siding, fretwork, gingerbread, stained glass, and a variety of textures and colours often combine to produce an exuberant effect.

ROMANESQUE REVIVAL
Flack Block (109)
This style was derived from the Romanesque architecture of medieval Europe. In the 1890s, a variant of this style, Richardsonian Romanesque (after American architect H.H. Richardson), became the preferred idiom for institutional and commercial buildings in North America. Round-arched windows, repeated in sequence, projecting piers with recessed spandrels, and the use of heavy rusticated masonry, often with intricate decoration, are distinguishing features.

SPANISH COLONIAL REVIVAL/MISSION STYLE
Kania Castle (364)
The architecture of the Spanish colonial period was revived in California in the early 1900s and found its way to Vancouver in the 1920s. In the United States, mission style (which is simpler in form) and Spanish colonial revival (more elaborate and ornamented) can be easily noted, but the differences become blurred in Vancouver. The characteristic features are white stucco walls, red tiled roofs, curved and shaped gables, round arches, arcades, wrought-iron balconies, and bas-relief or tiled ornament.

TUDOR REVIVAL
1678 Somerset Crescent
A style popular throughout the British Empire and beyond, Tudor revival recalled genteel living in the English country house manner. The characteristics of this nostalgic style are decorative half-timbering, especially in the gables (mimicking the heavy-timber frame and rubble stuccoed infill of buildings from the Elizabethan and Tudor periods). Complex roof forms and tall chimneys, often capped by chimney pots, complete the manor-house effect.

WEST COAST
D.H. Copp House, 4755 Belmont Avenue
Responding to the hilly, forested landscape of the West Coast, local postwar designers developed a style of domestic architecture variously derived from the international style, the prairie school of Frank Lloyd Wright, and Japanese house forms. Commonly using post-and-beam construction, the style, which can be expressed in many forms, makes use of stained or natural wood, concrete, gabled or shed roofs, and extensive glazing, in an intimate relationship with the local topography.

Glossary

Note: Words or phrases *in italics* are defined in a separate entry.

acanthus: floral decoration found in Greek and Roman architecture and often applied as a continuous horizontal band

Adamesque: a style named after Robert Adam, the 18th-century Scottish architect and interior designer known for his refined, picturesque *classicism*

aggregate: the granular component of *concrete* (usually sand or crushed stone)

arcade: a series of arches carried on *columns* or *pillars*, either free-standing or set in a wall; also a covered passage, often with a glass roof, and lined with shops on both sides

arch-and-spandrel motif: a wall treatment similar to a *pier-and-spandrel motif*, but in which the *piers* are joined at the top by arches

architrave: the main *beam* across the tops of *columns* in *classical* architecture; the lowest portion of an *entablature*

art nouveau: a European fin-de-siècle style characterized by free-flowing, plant-like forms and sinuous lines, often taken to bizarre extremes

ashlar: smooth, polished stonework set in regular blocks

atrium: a skylit, open space within a building, originally in Roman architecture

balustrade: a railing composed of posts (balusters) and a handrail

bargeboard: boards or other woodwork, usually decorated, fixed to the edges of a *gabled roof*

baroque: a 17th- and early 18th-century style of *classical* origin, curvaceous and often strongly composed and layered

bas-relief: a sculptural or cast panel on which the figures or ornament are partially raised from the background

Bauhaus: the 1920s school of architecture and design in Germany which promoted an avante-garde artistic socialism, paradoxically transformed in postwar North America as the corporate international style

bay: a window, door, or vertical repetition, comprising one visual division of a façade

bay window: a faceted, projecting window, usually three-sided

beam: a horizontal structural member. A girder is a large beam, often composed with additional structural supports fastened together.

bearing wall: a wall that supports all or some of the weight of the building above it

bellcast: see *eaves*

belle époque: the Edwardian era of gracious living, for those who could afford it, which ended with the First World War

belvedere: a small lookout tower; at ground level, a *gazebo*

bevelled siding: see *siding*

board-and-batten: see *siding*

bracket: a minor horizontal supporting member, below a *cornice*, for example, that projects from the vertical wall surface

buttress: an angled stone, brick, or timber support which gives the appearance of, and may actually be, holding up a wall, especially in Gothic architecture

Byzantine: the style of early medieval Christian architecture, in south-central Europe and later in Russia, characterized by flat domes and dark, enigmatic interiors

campanile: a bell tower (Italian)

cantilever: a *beam* that projects beyond a vertical support, usually diagonally braced

capital: the decorative head of an upright support or *column*

cartouche: an ornamental panel, sometimes with an inscription, and often elaborately framed

caryatid: a sculpted figure, often life-size or larger, usually female, supporting an *entablature*

cast iron: commonly used in the 19th century in place of stone or timber for *columns* and decorative features; in some cases, complete façades were assembled in cast iron.

cast stone: a kind of precast *concrete*, moulded to simulate natural stone and used as a substitute for it

cherub: a chubby childlike figure, often winged, in *Renaissance* art

chevron: a medieval, V-shaped pattern in Romanesque architecture; also an *art deco* feature

cladding: non-structural wall treatment applied to frame buildings, from houses to skyscrapers

clapboard: see *siding*

classical, classicism: deriving from the architecture of ancient Greece or Rome; or (classic) deriving from any standard of excellence

classical order: a conventional arrangement of a *column* (or other supports) and its *entablature* in which the proportions and ornamental detail are fixed by tradition. The ancient Greek and Roman architects devised a number of specific orders, the most common being the *Doric, Ionic,* and *Corinthian.*

clerestory: the upper window of a building, if treated separately from the main façade, providing high light to the interior

colonette: see *post*

colonnade: a procession of *columns* carrying arches or an *entablature*

column: see *post*

composition siding: see *siding*

concrete: a mixture of cement, *aggregate* (usually sand and gravel), and water that hardens and attains great compressive strength. When used structurally it is usually reinforced by being poured around steel rods or mesh to give it tensile strength as well. Concrete may be poured into forms (shuttering), usually of wood, directly in place in a structure, or it may be precast away from the site and then placed into position. Concrete blocks are precast and used as building blocks.

corbel: a kind of *bracket* composed of a single projecting block or of several courses of masonry

Corinthian order: the most ornate *classical order*, distinguished by foliated *capitals*

cornice: the uppermost portion of an *entablature*, often used in isolation as the projecting horizontal decorative element at the top of a building

crenellations: perpendicular indentations in a *parapet,* originally slits for guns

cresting: a decorative band at the top of a building; often a row of *finials*

crowstep gable: a *gable* in Scottish or Scandinavian architecture with sides composed as stone 'steps'

cupola: a small dome crowning a roof or other feature

curtain wall: an exterior wall that is

fastened to a *frame* and has no structural function; it supports only its own weight

density transfer: the transfer (by sale) of unrealized development (density) rights, permitted by *zoning*, from one property to another, usually as a means of preserving a historic building on the transferor's property

Doric order: the oldest *classical order*, with heavy, *fluted columns* and plain *capitals*

dormer: a window projecting from a sloping roof

eaves: the projecting edges of a roof. Bellcast eaves are those that curve outwards like the flanges of a bell.

eaves gallery: a row of columns framing *clerestory* windows or an arcaded space directly below a *cornice*

eclectic: architectural design that mixes sources from different historical periods

entablature: the decorated horizontal member directly above a *column* or other support; in *classical* architecture the entablature is composed of an *architrave*, a *frieze*, and a *cornice*

expressionism: an early 20th-century northern European style related to *art nouveau* and characterized by exaggerated angles

fanlight: a radiating window, usually above a door, in Georgian architecture

fenestration: the arrangement of windows on a façade

finial: a spiky ornament at the top of a *cupola*, turret, or other high element

fireproofed steel: structural steel encased in *concrete*, asbestos, or other fireproof material to prevent it from softening in the event of a fire

flatiron: a building that is triangular in plan

floor-space ratio (FSR): the ratio of the total floor area of a building to the area of its site; used in *zoning* as a means of controlling building size and density

fluting: repeated concave grooves running vertically up a *column* or *pilaster*

frame: the structural skeleton of a building; as an adjective, a timber structure

fretwork: a band of geometric, maze-like ornament in Greek and Chinese architecture

frieze: the middle portion of an *entablature*, or any horizontal decorated band, whether or not below a *cornice*

futurism: an anarchic Italian movement (c. 1914) which glorified technology, modern architecture, and transportation

gable: the triangular portion of a wall at the end of a pitched roof

gabled roof: a roof that slopes on two sides

galleria: an Italian *arcade* or any arcade, particularly a grand one, with galleries on more than one level; also a term now used to dignify a shopping mall

garden city: an early 20th-century ideal which sought to beautify cities with planned, leafy, communities; not unrelated to the Victorian arts and crafts movement in England

gargoyle: traditionally a water spout projecting from a roof parapet, carved as a grotesque animal or human figure, especially in Gothic architecture

garland: a carved or moulded hanging arrangement of fruit or leaves set in a panel; also known as a festoon

gazebo: an open section of a building or an open, separate, usually semicircular outbuilding

gingerbread: any elaborate wooden ornament; often refers to decorated *bargeboard*

girder: see *beam*

hacienda: a Spanish term for a large estate or house, broadly *classical* with overhanging tile roofs

hammerbeam: in a roof structure, a horizontal timber that projects from the wall as a *bracket* on which the arch timbers are supported; or a general name for this kind of roof structure

hipped roof: a roof that slopes on four sides

historicism: a 19th-century term describing contemporary revival of past architectural styles

hood moulding: a *moulding* located at the top of a window to deflect rainwater; often horizontal

Ionic order: a *classical order*, the *capital* of which is composed of two or four spiral scrolls

infill: new construction on an undeveloped portion of a property occupied by an existing building

iron: is either *cast* in a mould, giving it compressive strength (and hence generally used for *posts*) or *wrought* by being hammered and rolled, giving it greater tensile strength (and hence used for *beams* as well as decoratively)

Italianate: generally a 19th-century style of picturesque *classicism* with broad cornice overhangs, repeated (usually arched) windows, and, often, a *campanile*

Jacobean: an early 17th-century style in Britain identified by heavily *mullioned* windows, Flemish *gables*, heavy wood-panelled interiors, and flattened *cupolas*

lancet window: a tall, narrow window with a pointed arch; characteristic of the Gothic (and Gothic revival) style

lantern: a small turret or *cupola* with windows on all sides, surmounting a dome

lintel: a small *beam* set directly above a door or window

low-tech: a modern vernacular using basic, easily manufactured materials

machicolations: a row of *corbels* supporting a projecting wall mid-way up a medieval defensive structure; through downward-facing openings between the corbels defenders could pour boiling oil upon attackers

mansard: a steep roof with double-sloped sides and a flat peak, especially in French Second Empire style, often with ornamented dormers

Miesian: related to the architecture of German-American Ludwig Mies van der Rohe; a variant of the international style insistent upon the emphatic expression of structure through regular and perpendicular compositional elements

minaret: a tall, slender tower on a mosque

mock Tudor: a less than flattering term for the style of Tudor England as revived in the 19th and 20th centuries, notably on houses with country manor pretensions

modernism: the architecture of the mid-20th century; often called the international style

moulding: a decorative element, usually a horizontal band, that projects from the surface of a wall

mullion: vertical unit dividing glazed areas in a window

neocolonial: reviving a colonial style of architecture

oriel window: a *bay window* projecting from above ground-floor level, often continuing up a façade and repeated in each bay

palazzo: Italian palace, mansion, or ornate block of flats; particularly the large dwellings built by 15th-century Florentine merchant dynasties

Palladian: related to the buildings of the 16th-century architect Andrea Palladio, or to the 18th-century English revival of his style

palmette: a fan-shaped ornament in the form of a palm leaf

parapet: a portion of wall that projects above a roof

parquet: hardwood flooring laid in a repeat pattern of small, thin pieces

pediment: the triangular section above a *portico* or window, often containing sculptural groups, and sometimes curved or 'broken,' i.e., with the upper or lower centre removed

pier: see *post*

pier-and-spandrel motif: a wall treatment that emphasizes the play between vertical *piers* and horizontal *spandrels*

pilaster: see *post*

pillar: see *post*

pilotis: a French term, characteristic of Swiss-French architect Le Corbusier, describing structural *concrete posts* exposed at ground- to second-floor level on modernist buildings

planar: descriptive of a building that is flat or with few projections

porte-cochère: a covered entrance porch for vehicles

portico: a large columned entrance porch, open or partly enclosed, normally *classical* in style, supporting a *pediment*

post: any upright support. The word is most often used in a general sense (e.g., *post-and-beam* construction) or in specific reference to timber supports. Pillar is a somewhat archaic word synonymous with post. A pier is a post of square or rectangular section, usually of masonry. A column is a post of circular section; a steel member used vertically is also called a column. A colonette is a small column. A pilaster is a shallow rectangular upright support set into a wall and used mainly as decoration.

post-and-beam: a building system that emphasizes the regular use of horizontal (or slightly sloping) and vertical structural members

quatrefoil: a decorative form characterized by four lobes

Renaissance: the *rinascimento* or rebirth of *classical* art and architecture in 15th-century Italy and elsewhere in Europe

reticulated: patterned, in a net-like, intersecting manner, sometimes with relief or recessed elements

rococo: a delicate late *baroque* style applied to interior design rather than architecture

rose window: a circular window, usually on a church, with segmented *tracery* arranged like the petals of a flower

rotunda: a building with a circular plan, usually domed and occasionally enclosed by a *colonnade*. It can also mean a circular room or staircase, also domed, especially in *Palladian* architecture.

roughcast: stucco with a rough finish

rusticated: roughened for a rustic effect; usually refers to stonework composed of heavy blocks roughly chipped on the exposed side, giving a deep texture to façades, usually on the ground floor

Scottish baronial: originally a 16th-century style characterized by *crowstep gables* and Loire *château* turreted features, popularly revived in Scotland and elsewhere in the 19th century

scrollwork: ornament in the form of parchment partly unrolled or a lightly inscribed flourish or motif

secessionist: a style developed by a group of artists and architects in fin-de-siècle Vienna who rebelled against the *historicism* of the late Victorian era

Second Empire: the style of mid-19th century France, especially Paris, up until 1870; a pompous *neoclassicism* marked by ostentatious detail and capacious *mansard* roofs

segmental arch: an arch whose profile comprises an arc smaller than a semicircle

seismic: pertaining to structural design for earthquake resistance

shaft: the vertical portion of a *column* between the base and the *capital*

shed roof: a roof that slopes in one direction only

shiplap: see *siding*

siding: a facing material applied to the outside of a wood-framed building to make it weatherproof. Several kinds of wood siding are common in Vancouver. Shiplap consists of horizontally laid boards with notched edges that interlock; the face of each board is parallel to the face of the wall. Clapboard (or bevelled siding) consists of bevelled boards laid horizontally and overlapping at each edge; the face of each board is oblique to the wall. Board-and-batten siding is composed of vertically applied boards whose joints are covered by narrow strips (battens). Shingles may also be used as siding. Materials other than wood are often employed. Composition siding is made of asphalt, asbestos, or synthetic materials often imitating brick or shingle. Metal siding is usually composed of aluminum or galvanized steel.

spandrel: the portion of wall that appears between adjacent vertical supports directly below a window or between a window and an arch below

steel frame: a construction technique developed in the late 19th century which, with the invention of the elevator, led to skyscraper design

string-course: a horizontal row (course) in a masonry wall that contrasts with the general wall treatment

strip windows: a horizontal row of windows with common sills and heads and separated only by narrow *mullions*

terracotta: fired clay (literally 'baked earth') shaped in a mould and frequently glazed after firing; particularly popular as a decorative cladding on late Victorian, Edwardian, and art deco architecture

tongue-and-groove: a method of connecting pieces of wood in which a tongue in one piece is inserted into a groove in the other

tracery: interlacing on the upper part of a panel, screen, or window; usually Gothic and occasionally applied to ceilings

trefoil: a decorative form characterized by three lobes

Tuscan order: a *classical order* characterized by *capitals* that are less weighty than the *Doric*, and usually having a smooth *shaft*

Vancouver Special: a bland mass-built house type, introduced in the late 1960s, which is two storeys high with a low-pitched *gable* facing the street. The living quarters are all on the upper floor; a garage, utility rooms, and perhaps an 'in-law suite' are at grade.

vaulted: a ceiling or roof arched in a semicircular, pointed, or other fashion

view corridor: a planning term for a vista, usually framed by, and at the end of, a street

window head: the solid member at the top of a window

wrought iron: *iron* hand-beaten into the desired form. In appearance, wrought iron's thin strips and flakes are lighter and more delicate than the uniform finish of *cast iron*, with which it is often confused.

zoning: restrictions on building development by authorities (usually municipal governments) to control the use, site coverage, bulk, height, and other features of buildings

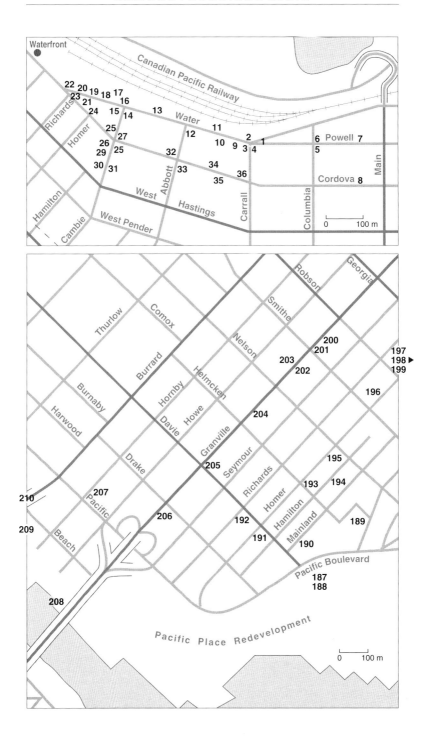

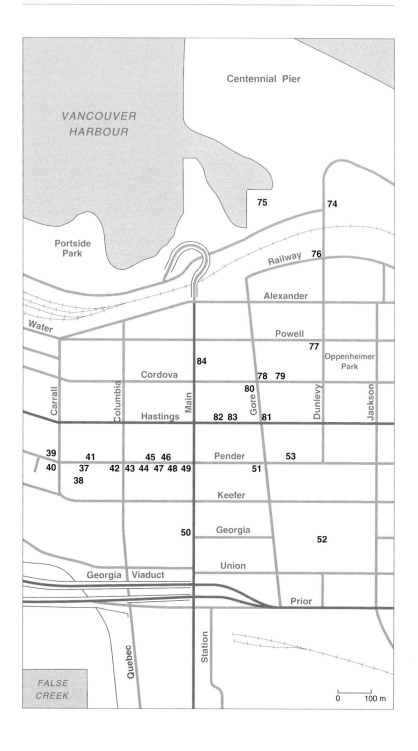

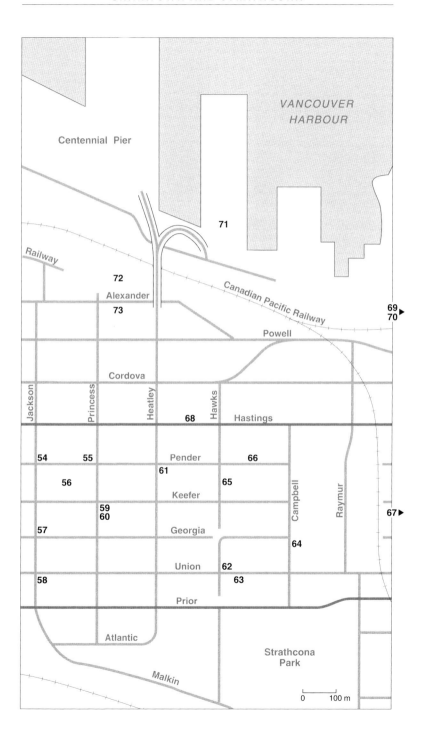

VANCOUVER HARBOUR

Centennial Pier

71

Railway

72

Alexander

73

Canadian Pacific Railway

Powell

69
70

Cordova

Jackson

Princess

Heatley

Hawks

68

Hastings

54   55

Pender

66

56

61

65

Keefer

59
60

Campbell

Raymur

67

57

Georgia

64

Union

62

58

63

Prior

Atlantic

Strathcona
Park

Malkin

0   100 m

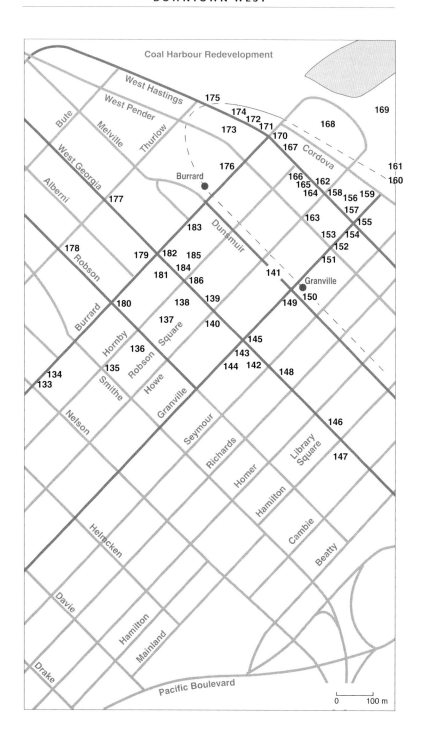

Coal Harbour Redevelopment

West Hastings

West Pender

175

174
172 171
173

169

168

Bute

Melville

Thurlow

170
167 Cordova

West Georgia

176

161
160

Alberni

Burrard

166
165 162
164 158 156 159
157

177

163

155

183

Dunsmuir

153 154
152

178

182 185

151

Robson

179

184
181 186

141

149 150

Granville

Burrard

180

138 139

137

140

145

143
144 142 148

Hornby

136

Robson Square

135

Howe

Smithe

Granville

134
133

Nelson

Seymour

146

Richards

147

Homer

Library Square

Hamilton

Helmcken

Cambie

Beatty

Davie

Hamilton

Mainland

Drake

Pacific Boulevard

0   100 m

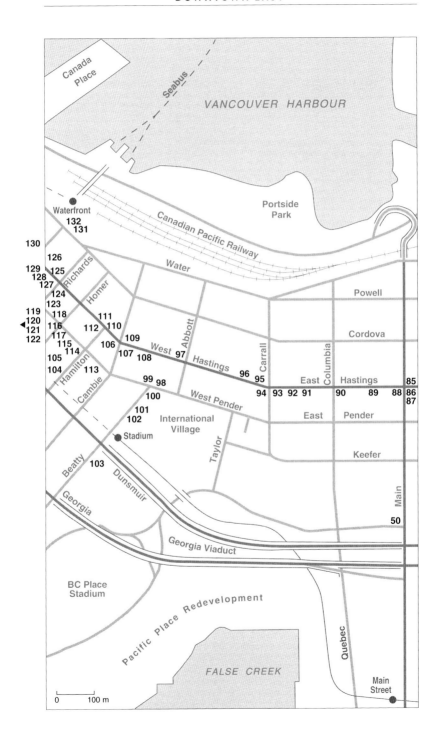

Canada Place

Seabus

VANCOUVER HARBOUR

Portside Park

Waterfront
132
131

Canadian Pacific Railway

130

126
129 125
128
127
124
123
119 118
120 116
121 117
122 115
105
104

Richards

Homer

Water

111
112 110
106 109
107 108

Powell

Cordova

Abbott

West 97 Hastings

96

East Columbia Hastings

85

94 93 92 91 90 89 88 86
87

Carrall

99 98
100
101
102

Hamilton

Cambie

113

West Pender

International Village

Taylor

Stadium

East Pender

Keefer

Beatty

103

Dunsmuir

Georgia

Georgia Viaduct

Main

50

BC Place Stadium

Pacific Place Redevelopment

Quebec

FALSE CREEK

Main Street

0   100 m

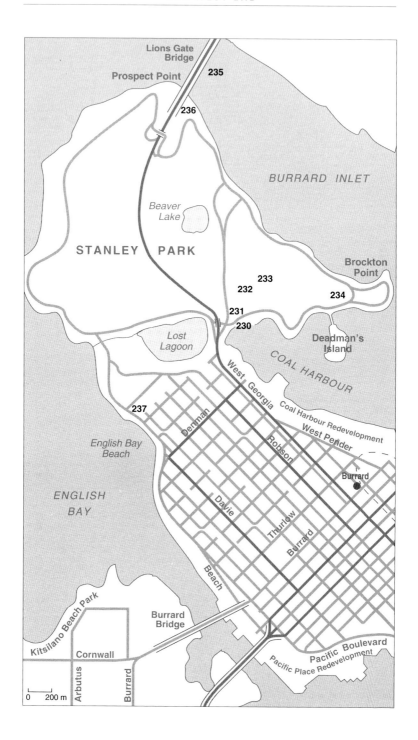

Lions Gate
Bridge

Prospect Point

235

236

BURRARD INLET

Beaver
Lake

STANLEY PARK

Brockton
Point

233

232

234

231

230

Lost
Lagoon

Deadman's
Island

COAL HARBOUR

West Georgia

237

Denman

Coal Harbour Redevelopment

West Pender

Robson

English Bay
Beach

Burrard

ENGLISH
BAY

Davie

Thurlow

Burrard

Beach

Kitsilano Beach Park

Burrard
Bridge

Pacific Boulevard

Cornwall

Pacific Place Redevelopment

Arbutus

Burrard

0   200 m

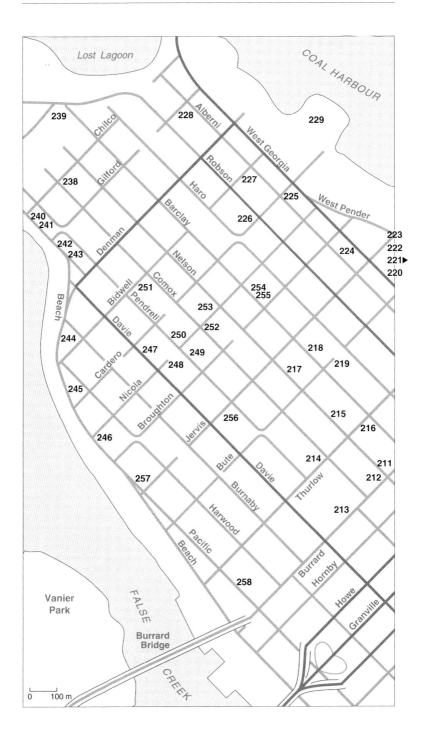

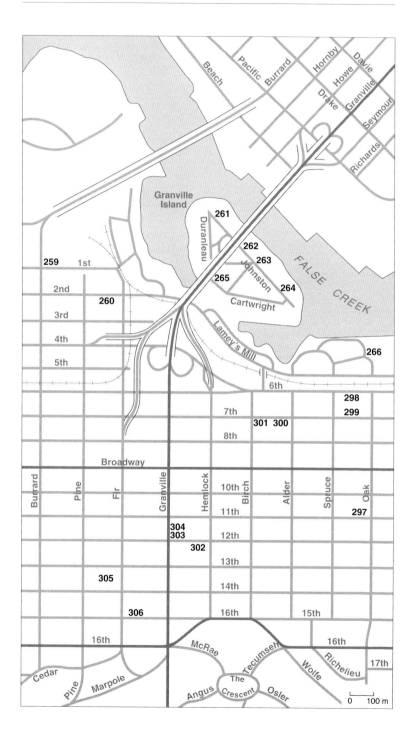

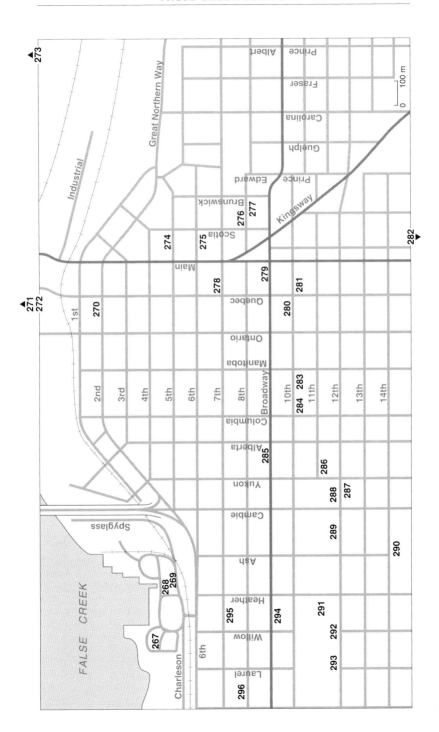

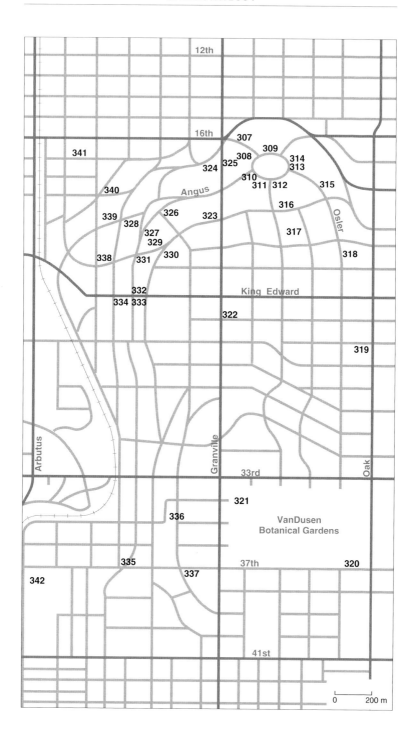

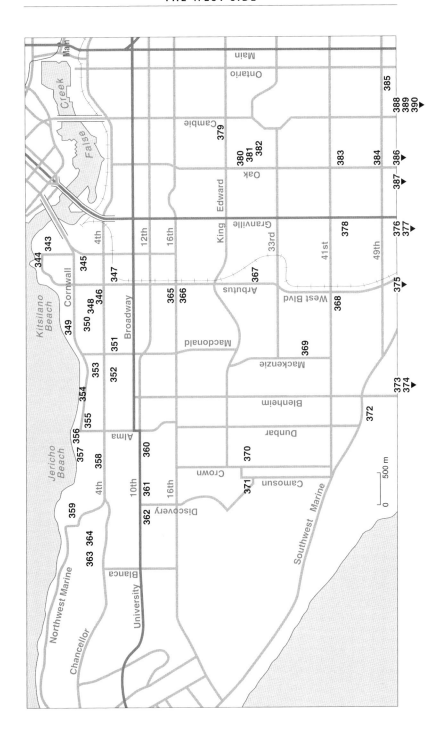

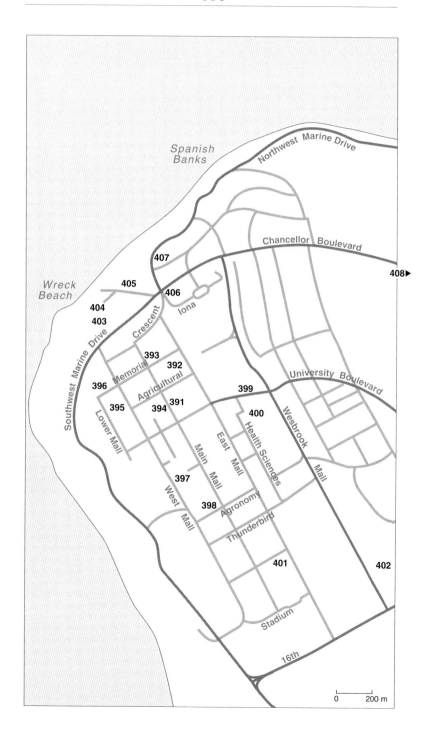

Spanish Banks

Northwest Marine Drive

Chancellor Boulevard

408▶

407

Wreck Beach

405

406

Iona

404

403

Crescent

Southwest Marine Drive

393

Memorial

392

Agricultural

396

395

394

391

Lower Mall

University Boulevard

399

400

Wesbrook Mall

East Mall

Health Sciences

Main Mall

397

West Mall

398

Agronomy

Thunderbird

401

402

Stadium

16th

0   200 m

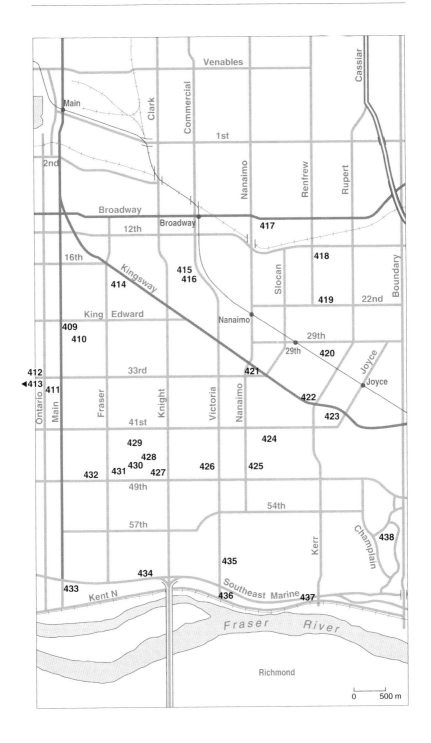

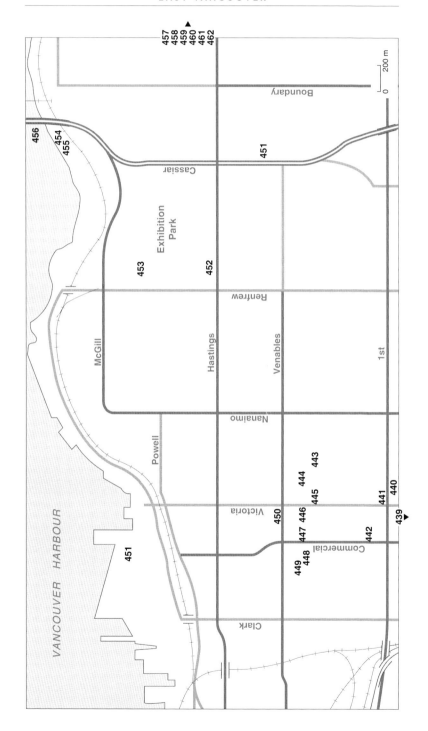

457
458
459
460
461
462

200 m

0

Boundary

456

454
455

451

Cassiar

Exhibition
Park

453

452

Renfrew

McGill

Hastings

Venables

1st

Nanaimo

Powell

444

443

445

441

440

Victoria

450

447 446

442

439

449
448

Commercial

VANCOUVER HARBOUR

451

Clark

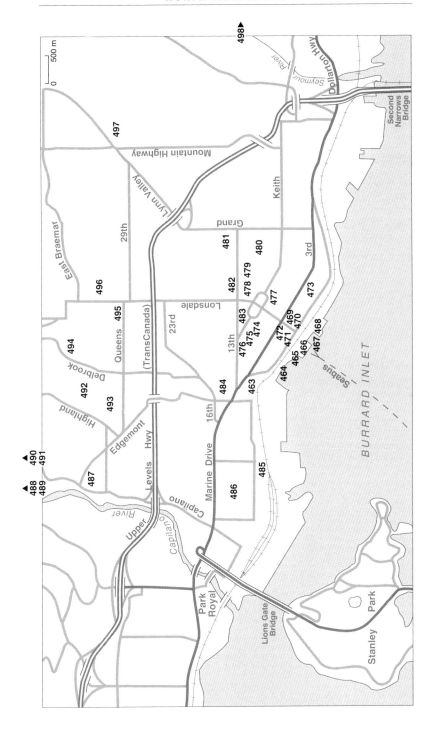

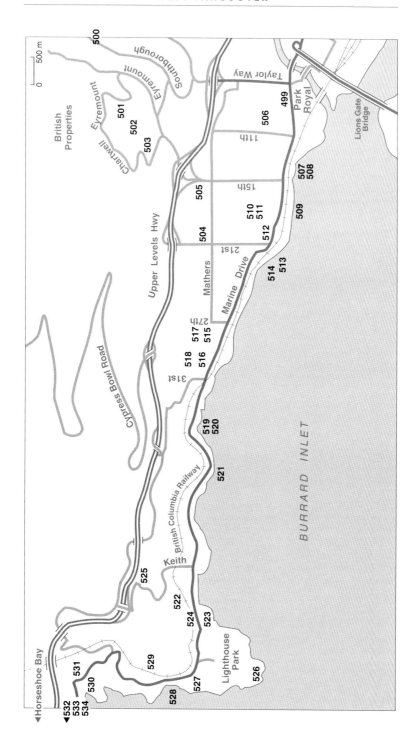

Bibliography

Allen Parker and Associates. 1986. *Vancouver Heritage Inventory: Summary Report.* Vancouver: City of Vancouver

Architectural Institute of British Columbia. [1992]. *The Map of Vancouver Architecture.* Vancouver: Architectural Institute of BC

Banham, Reyner. 1986. *A Concrete Atlantis: U.S. Industrial Architecture and European Modern Architecture.* Cambridge, MA: MIT Press

Barrett, Anthony A. and Rhodri Windsor Liscombe. 1983. *Francis Rattenbury and British Columbia.* Vancouver: UBC Press

Bodnar, Diana. 1982. *City of Vancouver: Heritage Inventory of Vancouver Schools.* Vancouver: City of Vancouver

Cawker, Ruth and William Bernstein. 1988. *Contemporary Canadian Architecture.* Toronto: Fitzhenry & Whiteside

Davis, Charles H., ed. 1973. *The Vancouver Book.* Vancouver: J. J. Douglas

– . 1990. *Reflections: One Hundred Years: A Celebration of the District of North Vancouver's Centennial.* Vancouver: Opus Productions

Eaton, Leonard K. 1971. *The Architecture of Samuel Maclure.* Victoria: Art Gallery of Greater Victoria

Edwards, Gregory. 1991. *Hidden Cities: Art and Design in Architectural Details of Vancouver and Victoria.* Vancouver: Talon Books

Ewert, Henry. 1986. *The Story of the British Columbia Electric Company.* Vancouver: Whitecap Books

Fleming, John, Hugh Honour, and Nikolaus Pevsner. 1991. *The Penguin Dictionary of Architecture.* 4th ed. London: Penguin

Foundation Group Designs. 1988. *The Ambitious City: City of North Vancouver Heritage Inventory.* City of North Vancouver

– . 1988. *District of North Vancouver Heritage Inventory.* District of North Vancouver

– . 1988. *West Vancouver Heritage Inventory.* District of West Vancouver

– . 1991. *Versatile Pacific Shipyards Heritage Survey.* City of North Vancouver

Franklin, Douglas. 1981. 'The Competition for the Design of the University of British Columbia,' *West Coast Review* 15 (4):49-57

Gibson, Edward M. 1971. 'The Impact of Social Belief on Landscape Change: A Geographical Study of Vancouver.' PhD dissertation, University of British Columbia

Gourley, Catherine. 1988. *Island in the Creek: The Granville Island Story.* Madeira Park:

Harbour Publishing

Gowans, Alan. 1966. *Building Canada: An Architectural History of Canadian Life*. Toronto: Oxford University Press

— . 1986. *The Comfortable House: North American Suburban Architecture, 1890-1930*. Cambridge, MA: MIT Press

Greater Vancouver Illustrated. 1908. Vancouver: Dominion Illustrating Company

Gutstein, Donald. 1975. *Vancouver Ltd*. Toronto: James Lorimer

Hardwick, Walter G. 1974. *Vancouver*. Toronto: Collier Macmillan

Hitchcock, Henry Russell. 1971 (1st ed. 1958). *Architecture of the Nineteenth and Twentieth Centuries*. London: Penguin

Holdsworth, Deryck W. 1977. 'House and Home in Vancouver: Images of West Coast Urbanism, 1886-1929.' In G.A. Stelter and Alan F.J. Artibise (eds.), *The Canadian City*. Pp. 186-211. Toronto: McClelland & Stewart

— . 1986. 'Cottages and Castles for Vancouver Home-Seekers,' *BC Studies* 69-70:11-32

Jacobs, Jane. 1961. *The Life and Death of Great American Cities*. New York: Random House

Kalman, Harold. 1978. *Exploring Vancouver 2*. Vancouver: UBC Press

Kluckner, Michael. 1984. *Vancouver the Way It Was*. Vancouver: Whitecap Books

— . 1990. *Vanishing Vancouver*. Vancouver: Whitecap Books

McAlester, Virginnia and Lee. 1991 (1st ed. 1984). *A Field Guide to American Houses*. New York: Alfred A. Knopf

MacDonald, Bruce. 1992. *Vancouver: An Illustrated History*. Vancouver: Talon Books

Mattison, David. 1986. *Eyes of a City: Early Vancouver Photographers, 1886-1900*. Vancouver: Vancouver City Archives

Morley, Alan. 1969. *Vancouver: From Milltown to Metropolis*. Vancouver: Mitchell Press

Munroe, Doris. 1972. 'Public Art in Vancouver.' MA thesis, University of British Columbia

Nicol, Eric. 1970. *Vancouver*. Toronto: Doubleday

O'Kiely, Elizabeth, ed. 1970. *Gastown Revisited*. Vancouver: Community Arts Council

'100 years of B.C. Living.' 1958. *Western Homes* (January):6-43

Ormsby, Margaret A. 1958. *British Columbia: A History*. Toronto: Macmillan

Palmer, Bernard C. 1928. 'Development of Domestic Architecture in British Columbia,' *Journal of the Royal Architectural Institute of Canada* 5:405-16

Pevsner, Nikolaus. 1960. *Pioneers of Modern Design*. London: Penguin

Pratt, C.E. 1947. 'Contemporary Domestic Architecture in British Columbia.' *Journal of the Royal Architectural Institute of Canada* 24:179-98

Roy, Patricia. 1980. *Vancouver: An Illustrated History*. Toronto: James Lorimer

Segger, Martin. 1986. *In Search of Appropriate Form: The Buildings of Samuel Maclure*. Victoria: Sono Nis

Vancouver Art and Artists, 1931-1983. 1983. Vancouver: Vancouver Art Gallery

Vancouver City Planning Department. 1974-5. *Vancouver's Heritage*. 2 vols. Vancouver: City of Vancouver

Wade, Jill. 1991. 'Citizens in Action.' PhD dissertation, Simon Fraser University

Walden, Phyllis Sarah. 1947. 'A History of West Vancouver.' MA thesis, University of British Columbia

Ward, Robin. 1990. *Robin Ward's Vancouver*. Madeira Park: Harbour Publishing

Watt, Robert D. 1980. *Rainbows on Our Walls: Art and Stained Glass in Vancouver*. Vancouver: Vancouver Museum

Whiffen, Marcus. 1969. *American Architecture since 1780: A Guide to the Styles*. Cambridge, MA: MIT Press

Woodward-Reynolds, Kathleen Marjorie. 1943. 'A History of the City and District of North Vancouver.' MA thesis, University of British Columbia

Sensuous sculptural effects

United Grain Growers elevator

A superb neoclassical palazzo

Crédit Foncier Building

Index

BUILDINGS AND OTHER STRUCTURES

Set in *Gill Sans* by George Vaitkunas

Printed and bound in Canada by
  D.W. Friesen & Sons Ltd.

Copy-editing: Holly Keller-Brohman

Proofreading: Stacy Belden

Cartography: Eric Leinberger

Photo printing: Steve Ray

Book design: Robin Ward

Bank of Montreal (detail)